Now
& Again

Now
&Ag

ain

Go-To Recipes, Inspired Menus + Endless Ideas for Reinventing Leftovers

Julia Turshen

Photography by David Loftus

CHRONICLE BOOKS
SAN FRANCISCO

Library of Congress Cataloging-in-Publication Data

Names: Turshen, Julia, author. | Loftus, David, photographer (expression)
Title: Now & again / by Julia Turshen ; photographs by David Loftus.
Other titles: Now and again
Description: San Francisco : Chronicle Books, 2018. | Includes
    bibliographical references and index.
Identifiers: LCCN 2017040842 | ISBN 9781452164922 (hardcover : alk. paper)
Subjects: LCSH: Cooking. | Cooking (Leftovers) | LCGFT: Cookbooks.
Classification: LCC TX714 .T8785 2018 | DDC 641.5—dc23 LC record available
at https://lccn.loc.gov/2017040842

Manufactured in China

Cover photograph by Jen May
Prop styling by Rebecca Bartoshesky and Julia Turshen
Food styling by Tyna Hoang, Caroline Lange, and Julia Turshen
Designed by Vanessa Dina
Typesetting by Howie Severson

10 9 8 7 6 5 4 3 2 1

Chronicle books and gifts are available at special quantity discounts to
corporations, professional associations, literacy programs, and other
organizations. For details and discount information, please contact our
premiums department at corporatesales@chroniclebooks.com or at
1-800-759-0190.

Chronicle Books LLC
680 Second Street
San Francisco, California 94107
www.chroniclebooks.com

For Grace, whom I fell in love
with then and do again and again . . .

Winter

BRUNCH FOR A CROWD 81

Sheet Pan Frittata with
Roasted Mushrooms + Ricotta 82

Spiced Banana Brown Bread 85

Shredded Cabbage Salad with Feta + Herbs 87

Cantaloupe with Lime + Salt 88

*It's Me Again: Ricotta Frittata Sandwiches,
Banana Bread French Toast, Couscous +
Cabbage Salad, Little Cabbage Hand Pies,
Easiest Cantaloupe Sorbet 89*

CHILI + CORNBREAD LUNCH 91

Chicken + Black-Eyed Pea Chili 92

Skillet Cornbread with Cheddar + Scallions 93

Romaine + Celery Salad
with Buttermilk Ranch Dressing 96

Caramelized Bananas
with Sour Cream + Brown Sugar 98

*It's Me Again: Chili Nachos,
Cornbread Stuffing, Spicy Stir-Fried
Lettuce + Celery with Garlic 99*

STEAK HOUSE DINNER FOR VEGETARIANS 101

Maple Syrup Old-Fashioneds 102

Stuffed Mushrooms with
Walnuts, Garlic + Parsley 103

Iceberg Wedge Salad with Pickled Shallots 105

Charred Broccoli with Capers + Lemon 106

Double-Baked Potatoes with
Horseradish + Cheddar 107

Black Forest Cake 109

*It's Me Again: Penne ai Fungi; Broccoli
Fritters; Superrich Potato Soup;
Crispy, Cheesy Potato Cakes 113*

FEAST OF THE ALMOST SEVEN FISHES 115

Crab Toasts with Lemon + Red Chile 117

Bagna Cauda with Endive + Fennel 118

Spaghetti with Scallops, Squid + Shrimp 119

Boozy Lemon Slushies 122

*It's Me Again: Bagna Cauda Caesar Dressing,
Roasted Fennel + Endive,
Roasted Red Cabbage with Anchovy +
Pine Nuts, Crab Cakes,
Korean-Style Cold Seafood Salad,
Boozy Lemon Pound Cake 123*

A NOT-KOSHER JEWISH CHRISTMAS 125

Crispy Scallion + Sesame Pancakes 126

Oven-Steamed Fish with
Crispy Garlic + Red Chile Oil 130

Stir-Fried Roasted Eggplant with Pork 133

Baby Bok Choy with Sesame Sauce 134

Takeout Rice

Orange Wedges

*It's Me Again: Fish + Crispy Garlic Fried Rice,
Cold Rice Noodle + Bok Choy Salad,
Eggplant + Pork Potstickers, Leftover Rice 135*

Spring

Summer

Now & Again *has three goals.*

One is to dismantle the idea that making a full meal has to be both difficult and expensive. The second is to show how leftovers can be an invitation to really fun, inventive cooking. The third and final is to make sure you have all of the tools you need—the inspiration and information—to gather people around your table because that is the best part about home cooking.

But first I owe you some full disclosure. *Now & Again* started as a completely different book. Based on my love of leftovers, I had an idea to write a book about reinventing them called . . . wait for it . . . *It's Me Again.* Cooking with leftovers makes me so excited: *you're already halfway there!* I was very thrilled about the idea. I was also sure it wasn't *enough.* I wanted to give you not only ideas for how to reinvent leftovers but also recipes for what to make in the first place.

In thinking about what these recipes would be, I kept coming back to a question a lot of friends and family seemed to be asking me: *what should I serve with it?* This question also ties into what and how I really cook at home every day. I rarely ever cook just a single thing. Even if it's just a salad next to a roast chicken or a toasted pita underneath scrambled eggs with a little yogurt spooned on top, I tend not to cook stand-alone recipes, but rather a few simple things that all complement one another and make the sum greater than the parts. I am all about what goes with what.

For me, creating menus isn't about entertaining, which can feel intimidating. It's about storytelling. There's always something(s) alongside the main thing on my table. And it's in the relationship those things share that full pictures get painted and stories are told. It could be as simple as meatballs with spaghetti, with maybe a little garlicky toast to sop up the sauce or a tangle of peppery arugula to add something green and to balance the whole thing. Each of those things is made better by the relationship it has with its friends. By assembling all of them, the meatballs and the salad and so on, I'm not just making food. I'm making a meal with a clear point of view and a story.

My forever goal for what I cook, eat, and for the recipes I write is to feel connected. I'm always searching for and celebrating this feeling. It doesn't matter to me if it's a fancy lobster dinner or an omelet at the diner (honestly, I prefer the latter). I am just as excited about the popcorn from the hardware store as I am about the spiciest fried chicken in Nashville, the most lovingly baked bread, and my family recipes handed down for generations. All of these things are connected to something. In preparing them and eating them, the experience becomes more than just food. It's tied to a feeling.

Food, after all, isn't just something we eat. It's a lens through which we can understand ourselves and all of the folks that came before us. It's also the lens through which we can, remarkably, better understand one another. Cooking is an easy way to connect with people, both those you know and those who are different from you, on a regular basis.

As a teenager, I wrote menus in the margins of my school notebooks. It was my favorite way to daydream. Those menus felt like little fantasies of the life I might one day lead, of the dishes I could make to celebrate special occasions and holidays, and of the ones I could stir up when comfort was needed. It was my way to imagine and connect with the world beyond my classroom. It was also a way to connect with myself and with the independent life I so very much wanted to live. As an adult, I can attest that bringing these menus to life for everyone I care so deeply about, and for all of the people I want to know better, gives me enormous joy and satisfaction.

This idea of connection, both with the dishes on the table and with the people sitting at it, is why I arranged this book by menus instead of stand-alone recipes. Some are incredibly easy, like the Simple Backpack Picnic Lunch on page 215 that is just sandwiches, some nectarines and nuts, and some cookies. It's not much cooking. But it's the perfect balance of things, each in relation to the other. It's also tied to a memory, and it's a way for me to evoke that memory. Food, in other words, is an effective way of chronicling life. For example, those particular sandwiches were the same ones my wife, Grace, and I had on a hike near our home in upstate New York. While I might not always immediately recall exactly where the trail was, I will always remember the sandwiches. And in remembering them, the whole day comes back to me.

Some menus in the book, like the one for Thanksgiving, are more involved. But no matter how few or how many components, each menu is built on food that's entirely doable. There are also timetables for each menu, so it's clear exactly what and how much you can make ahead, plus lots of thoughts throughout on things that go well with the menus that require no work whatsoever (like sometimes orange wedges are all you need after a big meal). There's even a list of great things to delegate on page 278.

And then, *It's Me Again*, which are all of the ways to reinvent the leftovers. Grace and I live in a small, rural town and eat almost all of our meals at home. Therefore, we always make a bit more than we can finish at a single sitting. Tomorrow's meals are always informed by what's left over from today and so on. It's proven to be a really relaxing, effective cycle, and we're always sure there's something good to eat. All of the recipes in this book come from that similar place of plenty, from the feeling that there is more than enough. And where there is more than enough, there are leftovers. And where there are leftovers, there are endless opportunities for reinvention. These suggestions are some of the most fun parts of the book. They're full of ideas for how to turn the leftovers into entirely new dishes that, as Grace says, "don't taste like the same thing again!" Note that all of these ideas for leftovers are applicable whether or not you made the original recipe. So, for example, if you're staring at some cooked chicken in your refrigerator and are feeling uninspired, turn to the Coronation Chicken Salad on page 61, or take your seemingly boring leftover broccoli and make the Broccoli Fritters on page 113. All of the recipes are categorized by type at the back of the book (page 280) to make referencing them extra easy.

There are no rules here. The full menus are there if you'd like to follow them. But it's also wonderful if you want to pick and choose recipes, maybe something from one menu paired with something from another. Or just make a single thing, call a friend to bring over a loaf of bread and a green salad, and call it a day. Whatever works for you works for me, so long as it means you're happy in your kitchen and you're providing yourself and the people you love with food that makes you all feel good.

Speaking of those people, one last thought from my friend and fellow cookbook author Nicole Taylor before we get into the kitchen. I was talking to her about how gathering people for a meal can make everyone feel connected and welcome and supported—all wonderful, positive things. And she asked me a question that fundamentally challenged and changed me: *when was the last time you had more than one person around your dining table who didn't look like you?* Cooking for someone is a powerful thing to do. Invite someone new over. Connection and change happen at the table, and you're all welcome at mine.

Autumn

SUNDAY MORNING
BANGLADESHI BREAKFAST

RED-CHECKERED TABLECLOTH
LATE SATURDAY LUNCH

CARD NIGHT ENCHILADAS

ROSH HASHANAH DINNER

NO STRESS THANKSGIVING

Sunday Morning Bangladeshi Breakfast

SCRAMBLED EGGS WITH CILANTRO + COCONUT CHUTNEY

WHOLE WHEAT + CUMIN FLATBREADS

MANGO WITH CARDAMOM SYRUP + PISTACHIOS

A few years ago, I got to work on *The Hot Bread Kitchen Cookbook*, a collection of recipes and stories from New York's Hot Bread Kitchen bakery. An intensive workforce development program that trains immigrant women facing economic insecurity, Hot Bread Kitchen offers bakers not only on-the-job skills but also all of the tools (like an English-as-a-second-language program and management lessons) they need to launch their own careers in food. In a beautiful, full-circle kind of way, all of the breads and baked goods the bakery produces are influenced by the women and the places they are from.

Working on the book not only taught me about great baking, from challah to *m'smen*, but also introduced me to some incredible people, including the unforgettable Lutfunnessa Islam. Born and raised in Bangladesh, Lutfunnessa was a political science teacher before immigrating to America, where she became a mother and then a trainee at Hot Bread Kitchen. She is now a production supervisor, trains new bakers, and also oversees the bakery's stand at the Jackson Heights Greenmarket (in Queens, one of the most culturally diverse neighborhoods in New York City, not to mention the country). Lutfunnessa is a ray of clever, fun light, and I really enjoyed getting to know her while working on the book.

(Continued)

UP TO 1 MONTH AHEAD

Make the flatbread dough, dust it with flour, wrap it in plastic wrap, place it in an airtight freezer bag, and freeze. Defrost in the refrigerator overnight and then let it come to room temperature before rolling out and cooking.

Make the cardamom syrup and store in a tightly capped jar in the refrigerator.

UP TO 1 WEEK AHEAD

Make the chutney and store in a tightly capped jar in the refrigerator.

UP TO 1 DAY AHEAD

Make and cook the flatbreads, wrap them in aluminum foil, and keep at room temperature. Warm them in a 300°F [150°C] oven (still wrapped in the foil) before serving. Or remove the foil, wrap the breads in a damp paper towel, and microwave for about 30 seconds before serving. Alternatively, make the dough and divide into portions as directed. Wrap in plastic wrap and refrigerate for up to 24 hours, then let the dough come to room temperature, roll it out, and cook just before serving.

The mangoes can be sliced and dressed with the syrup, then covered and refrigerated until serving.

LAST MOMENT

When your guests arrive, scramble the eggs, cook (or just warm) the flatbreads, and sprinkle the pistachios on the mangoes.

One especially memorable morning, I left my apartment around 5:30 a.m. to meet her at the bakery, and she taught me to make chapattis, the thin unleavened whole wheat flatbreads she had learned from her mother, followed by her perfect curried vegetables and stewed beef. Writing cookbooks is always a lot of fun, but sometimes it feels especially meaningful.

If you ever find yourself in Jackson Heights on a Sunday morning, go watch Lutfunnessa do her thing at the greenmarket. A true showwoman, she sells out of everything. Whenever I would go to see her there, I would always get lots of stuff like eggs and fresh herbs to bring home for making a breakfast I hoped she would approve of. Here it is.

Scrambled Eggs
with Cilantro + Coconut Chutney

SERVES 4

Scrambled eggs are probably what I eat most frequently, but they aren't much to write home about. This chutney is. It takes the eggs from ordinary to remarkable, and, here's the best part, it is as easy as throwing a bunch of things into a food processor and pressing the button. There's no cooking, just combining. It keeps well in an airtight container in the refrigerator for up to a week (it gets quite a bit thicker and loses a bit of its fresh, herby brightness, but it is still great), and it's also good on roast chicken, grilled fish, broiled lamb, griddled *halloumi* cheese, or roasted sweet potatoes. If you don't like cilantro, substitute fresh mint.

2 large handfuls of fresh cilantro leaves (a little bit of stem is fine!)

1 Tbsp peeled and minced or grated fresh ginger

½ tsp cumin seeds or ground cumin

½ cup [35 g] unsweetened flaked dried coconut

1½ tsp kosher salt

¼ cup [60 ml] coconut milk (full-fat or low-fat coconut milk will work)

1½ tsp fresh lime juice

8 eggs

2 Tbsp unsalted butter

In a food processor, combine the cilantro, ginger, cumin, dried coconut, and ½ tsp salt and pulse until the cilantro is finely chopped. Add the coconut milk and lime juice and pulse just to combine (you want the chutney to have a little texture, rather than be totally smooth). Set the chutney aside.

Crack the eggs into a large bowl and whisk until the whites and yolks are well blended. Add the remaining salt and whisk one more time.

In a large nonstick skillet over medium heat, melt the butter. Add the eggs and cook, stirring gently with a wooden spoon or heat-resistant spatula, until they are as set as you like them to be.

Transfer the eggs to a large platter. Serve the chutney either spooned on top or in a bowl on the side.

Whole Wheat + Cumin Flatbreads

SERVES 4

These flatbreads are a great introduction to making bread at home. It's a really forgiving recipe and incorporates some of the chapatti lessons I learned from Lutfunnessa, including how to make breads with all whole wheat flour that aren't too dense and how to cook them in a hot skillet, instead of in the oven, for ease, speed, and great charred flavor. If you don't love cumin, feel free to leave it out or to substitute another spice, such as fennel or caraway seeds. You could also add a handful of roughly chopped fresh cilantro to the dough.

1 tsp active dry yeast (about ½ standard packet)

¼ cup [60 ml] water, warmed to body temperature

½ cup [120 g] plain full-fat Greek yogurt

1½ Tbsp unsalted butter, melted and cooled

1½ tsp kosher salt

1 tsp sugar

½ tsp baking soda

1 tsp cumin seeds or ground cumin

1¼ cups [175 g] whole wheat flour, plus a bit more if needed

Check the expiration date on your yeast and make sure you're in the clear. Put the yeast and water into a large bowl and stir to combine. Let the mixture sit until the yeast is dissolved and the mixture is cloudy (almost like miso soup), about 5 minutes. A few tiny bubbles might appear on the surface, which is great, but it's also okay if they don't.

Add the yogurt, 1 Tbsp of the butter, the salt, sugar, baking soda, and cumin seeds and stir well to combine. The baking soda might cause the mixture to fizz a little, which just means it's working, so no need to worry. Add the flour and stir with a wooden spoon until everything comes together to form a dough (it will be sticky). If some of the flour doesn't mix in immediately, get in there with your hands and mix until it is absorbed.

Knead the dough in the bowl (press it with the heel of your hand and push it away from you, then immediately pull it back, folding the top back onto itself) for about 3 minutes. The dough should be nice and smooth and, honestly, it won't feel or look all that different from when you started kneading. But the kneading will help the gluten get going, and that's important to do, so please don't skip this step. If the dough sticks to your hands a lot as you're kneading, simply dust it with a little more flour.

(Continued)

Drizzle the dough with the remaining ½ Tbsp butter. Turn the dough to coat it with the butter and then cover the bowl with a kitchen towel. Set the dough aside to rise until it's soft, puffy, and slightly larger than when you first set it aside, about 1 hour. If there's a warm spot in your kitchen, put it there (inside a turned-off microwave is good).

Transfer the rested dough back to a clean work surface and use a knife to cut it into four equal pieces. Roll each piece into a small ball, then use a rolling pin to roll it out into a thin oval that measures about 6 in [15 cm] long. You shouldn't need any extra flour for this, but if the dough is sticking to the work surface or the rolling pin, dust it very lightly with flour.

Place a large cast-iron skillet over medium-high heat and let it get nice and hot. Place a flatbread in the hot pan and cook until the underside is nicely browned and charred in spots, 1 to 2 minutes. Flip the flatbread and cook until the second side is nicely browned, about 1 minute. (You can also use a stainless-steel skillet, but you might need to add a minute of cooking on one or both sides.)

Transfer the cooked flatbread to a warm platter or a napkin-lined basket to keep it warm, then repeat the process with the rest of the dough pieces. Serve the breads while still warm.

Mango with Cardamom Syrup + Pistachios

SERVES 4

Although there's often nothing better than ripe fruit served without fanfare, everything likes to be dressed up now and then. The combination of cardamom syrup and toasted pistachios is super simple and takes plain mango from uneventful to gorgeous, with flavors that are wonderful together. If you like the flavor of cardamom, make a double batch of the syrup and use it in your hot or iced tea for a chai-ish vibe.

6 green cardamom pods, crushed, or ½ tsp ground cardamom

Pinch of kosher salt

3 Tbsp packed light brown sugar

3 Tbsp water

2 large or 3 medium ripe, juicy mangoes, peeled, pitted, and sliced

3 Tbsp shelled pistachios, toasted and roughly chopped

In a small saucepan over medium heat, combine the cardamom, salt, brown sugar, and water. Bring to a boil, stirring to dissolve the sugar, about 1 minute. Turn off the heat and let the mixture cool to room temperature. Pour the syrup through a fine-mesh sieve into a small pitcher.

Arrange the mango slices artfully—but not too preciously—on a serving platter. Drizzle the cardamom syrup evenly over the slices and then sprinkle with the pistachios. Serve immediately or store for up to 1 day, covered and refrigerated.

It's Me Again

CURRIED SCRAMBLED EGG SALAD

Leftover scrambled eggs can be turned into egg salad. Let them cool to room temperature (which they probably already are if they're left over), put them into a bowl, and break them up with a spoon. Add a good shake of curry powder and then bind with as much mayonnaise as you like (egg salad is a very personal thing). Or you can use half mayonnaise and half plain Greek yogurt if you want to lighten things a bit. Taste and adjust the seasoning with salt and curry powder if needed. You can also add a big spoonful of the Cilantro + Coconut Chutney (or maybe it was already on the eggs, in which case, you're set). Delicious served on well-toasted leftover flatbreads or pita breads.

FLATBREAD PIZZA

Warm the flatbread in a microwave (wrap the bread in a damp paper towel) or toaster oven for about 30 seconds and then dress with toppings (perhaps tomato sauce and shredded mozzarella; ricotta, roasted garlic, and some sautéed spinach; or maybe spicy tomato sauce with thinly sliced prosciutto . . . whatever you like!). Broil in your toaster oven or regular oven until the toppings are melted, bubbling, and/or browned. Serve warm.

MANGO CHUTNEY

Combine a finely chopped red onion, about 1 Tbsp peeled and minced or grated fresh ginger, a minced garlic clove, and a little fat (olive oil, coconut oil, unsalted butter, or ghee would work equally well) in a medium skillet. Season with a good shake of curry powder and some red pepper flakes and then cook over medium heat until the aromatics are softened but not browned. Meanwhile, roughly chop the leftover mango. Once the aromatics have softened, add the mango, a large handful or two is ideal (with whatever syrup and pistachios are left), and a healthy splash of apple cider vinegar and simmer everything together for a few minutes to blend the flavors well. Taste and adjust the seasoning with salt and vinegar if needed. You can leave the chutney as is or you can purée it a little or a lot in a food processor. Cool to room temperature and store in a tightly capped jar in the refrigerator for up to a week. Serve with grilled or roasted meats (lamb and pork are especially nice) or tuck some into a grilled cheese sandwich. It's also great served on its own alongside a piece of sharp Cheddar for snacking or mixed with equal parts mayonnaise for a turkey or ham sandwich spread.

Red-Checkered Tablecloth
Late Saturday Lunch

GARLIC + ANCHOVY BUTTER TOASTS

ITALIAN FLAG BAKED PASTA

ARUGULA SALAD WITH LEMON, PINE NUTS + PECORINO

JODY'S PLUM BIBONADE

POLENTA + NUTELLA SANDWICH COOKIES

I spent twenty out of my first thirty years living in Manhattan (with a pit stop in Brooklyn when I met Grace, where she had lived for a dozen years). A couple of years ago, we moved about two hours north of the city. As a self-proclaimed "New Yorker for life," I can't quite believe how happy I am living in the country. How exactly did we end up in our little town? It's all thanks to a couple we know, Laura and Fabio. They're city-and-country folks who live an almost dual life working in fashion in the city and then running their orchard in the country.

Before Grace and I found our home, Laura and Fabio had us over to theirs for what turned out to be one of the most memorable lunches of my life. Nonna, Laura's mother, cooked. She set out wooden boards (that Fabio had made) topped with prosciutto and salami (that Fabio had made) and olives and then came the pasta (the sublime pasta!) made by Nonna with eggs from their chickens and local flour and topped with garlic and tomatoes grown on their farm, followed by small glasses filled with peaches (grown nearby) and cold white wine. I thought that was that, but then Laura's brother appeared with a bowl of gooseberries (that he had just picked) and Laura poured some maple syrup (from their own trees, naturally) over the berries and spooned some of the softest whipped cream imaginable on top. Hope, our dog, ran around with Bosco, their dog, and the weather was perfect. Grace and I, without even saying a thing to each other, knew that a different life than we ever imagined could be ours if we decided. This menu is an ode to that day.

UP TO 1 MONTH AHEAD	Make the cookie dough, roll it into a log in plastic wrap, place the whole thing in an airtight freezer bag, and freeze. Let the log sit at room temperature for about 30 minutes before slicing.
UP TO 3 DAYS AHEAD	Make the garlic and anchovy butter, wrap it in plastic wrap, and store in the refrigerator, then bring to room temperature before using. Slice and bake the cookies but do not fill, then store in a cookie tin at room temperature.
UP TO 1 DAY AHEAD	Make the baked pasta up to the point of baking and cover and store in the fridge.
UP TO A FEW HOURS AHEAD	Slice the fruit for the bibonade and sandwich the cookies with the filling. Toast the pine nuts, wash the arugula, and shave the cheese for the salad, then build the salad in the bowl with the dressing at the bottom and place a damp paper towel on top.
LAST MOMENT	Just before your guests arrive, mix together the bibonade and make the toasts. While everyone is enjoying those, pop the pasta in the oven and toss together the salad.

Garlic + Anchovy Butter Toasts

SERVES 6

The spread for these toasts is basically Caesar salad dressing in butter form. I mean . . . ! It's great swirled with spaghetti, melted over broiled or grilled shrimp, dotted over a pot of steamed clams, or tossed with roasted broccoli and/or cauliflower. You can put out other things to nosh on along with the toasts, like radishes and thinly sliced raw fennel, sliced salami, and olives. I love all of these items because they require no cooking.

4 Tbsp [55 g] unsalted butter, at room temperature

1 large garlic clove, minced

4 olive oil-packed anchovy fillets, minced

A large handful of fresh Italian parsley leaves (a little bit of stem is fine!), finely chopped

½ tsp kosher salt

6 thick slices country bread

In a small bowl, combine the butter, garlic, anchovies, parsley, and salt and mash everything together well with a fork. Once everything is roughly mixed, use a spoon to really whip the butter until it is nice and smooth and everything is evenly incorporated.

Toast the bread slices under the broiler, in batches in a toaster, or on a grill until they're as dark as you like them. While the toast is still warm, spread each one generously with the butter mixture. Serve the toasts warm, either as nice large pieces or cut into smaller bites (there are merits to both).

Italian Flag Baked Pasta

SERVES 6

Each of the components of this easy baked pasta can have a life of its own. The turkey-tomato sauce is an excellent and quick meat sauce that's perfect for weeknight dinners. It's great on pasta or polenta or just eaten solo alongside a pile of cooked, garlicky greens. Feel free to substitute ground beef, pork, or chicken for the turkey (or leave the meat out entirely if you're vegetarian or want to be for this meal). The spinach mixture can be stirred into scrambled eggs, turned into a toast topping (see page 39), or used as ravioli filling if you like making homemade pasta.

2 Tbsp olive oil

1 lb [455 g] ground dark-meat turkey

Kosher salt

Freshly ground black pepper

4 garlic cloves, minced

One 28-oz [794-g] can crushed tomatoes

3 leafy fresh basil sprigs, tough stems reserved and leaves roughly chopped

1 lb [455 g] short, ridged pasta (whatever type you like)

Two 10-oz [280-g] packages frozen spinach, defrosted, squeezed dry, and roughly chopped

1 cup [240 g] crème fraîche or sour cream

¼ tsp freshly grated nutmeg

¾ cup [75 g] finely grated Parmesan cheese

1 cup [100 g] coarsely grated mozzarella cheese

Preheat your oven to 400°F [200°C].

Get a large pot of water going on the stove top for your pasta. If it boils before you're ready to cook the pasta, just turn it down (better for it to wait for you than vice versa).

In a large, heavy pot over medium-high heat, warm the olive oil. Break up the turkey into small pieces, add it to the pot, and season aggressively with salt and pepper. Cook, stirring every now and then, until the meat is cooked through and very nicely browned and any liquid it released has evaporated, about 15 minutes. Add the garlic, tomatoes (along with their juice), basil stems, and another large pinch of salt and a few grinds of pepper. Give the whole mixture a good stir with a wooden spoon to scrape up any browned bits that are stuck to the bottom of the pot. Bring the mixture to a boil, lower the heat to a simmer, and cook the sauce until it is slightly reduced and smells wonderful, about 20 minutes. Remove and discard the basil stems. Turn off the heat and set the sauce aside.

At this point, your pasta water should be boiling. Salt it generously and add the pasta. Cook it until just al dente (remember it will bake for a while), about 1 minute less than the package instructs. Drain the pasta, add it to the pot with the tomato sauce, and stir well to combine.

(Continued)

While the pasta is cooking, put the spinach, crème fraîche, nutmeg, Parmesan, half of the mozzarella, and the chopped basil leaves into a large bowl. Sprinkle with 1 tsp salt and stir well to combine.

Spoon one-third of the sauced pasta into a 9-by-13-in [23-by-33-cm] baking dish and spread into an even layer. Dot the pasta with half of the spinach mixture and use a spoon or even just your clean hands to spread the spinach mixture in an even layer. Continue with half of the remaining pasta, all of the remaining spinach mixture, and then the final bit of pasta. Sprinkle the remaining mozzarella on top.

Bake the pasta, uncovered, until it is gorgeously browned and the edges are bubbling, about 30 minutes. Let it rest at room temperature for at least 15 minutes before serving. This resting time lets everything settle into place.

Arugula Salad with Lemon, Pine Nuts + Pecorino

SERVES 6

This salad is so simple it hardly needs a recipe. I love serving it with the baked pasta not only because it's so easy to make but also because the peppery greens and bright lemon juice help cut the richness of the pasta.

2 Tbsp fresh lemon juice

¼ cup [60 ml] extra-virgin olive oil

½ tsp kosher salt

9 oz [255 g] baby arugula

¼ cup [30 g] pine nuts, lightly toasted (see Note)

½ cup [50 g] thinly shaved pecorino cheese (a vegetable peeler is a good tool for this)

In a large salad bowl, whisk together the lemon juice, olive oil, and salt. Place the arugula on top. At this point you can cover the bowl with a kitchen towel and let it sit for a couple of hours at room temperature. Right before serving, gently toss everything together. Top with the pine nuts and cheese and serve immediately.

Note: To toast the pine nuts, put them into a dry skillet over medium heat and cook, stirring, until they're golden brown, about 2 minutes.

Jody's Plum Bibonade

SERVES 6

Working with Jody Williams to create *Buvette*, her book with recipes and stories from her restaurant of the same name, was one of my best work experiences. Not only is Jody incredibly funny (like, laugh-out-loud funny), kind, and generous, but she is also, more than anyone I know, in tune with the ability of food and drink to evoke a particular feeling. Working with her taught me so much, and I have carried many of those lessons into my life and into my kitchen. Some of these things are big ideas, like being free from the expected, and some are simple, like this bibonade.

Jody made up the term *bibonade* (another thing I like about Jody is her love for making up words), and it refers to a refreshing drink made of wine, sparkling water, ice, and fruit. It's sort of like a light sangria, and because it is only a little bit boozy, it's perfect for daytime drinking. Plus, it's easy to make for a crowd. Jody changes up the fruit and wine seasonally, so feel free to do the same. This particular riff uses plums because we're in the autumn chapter and stone fruits that grow in the area I live in hit their peak in early fall. But honestly, use any fruit you like and have fun. Other great combinations include halved grapes in rich white wine, raspberries in rosé, and peaches in dry white wine.

One 750-ml bottle dry white wine, preferably chilled

One 750-ml bottle seltzer or sparkling water, preferably chilled

1 orange

Ice cubes for serving

3 plums, pitted and thinly sliced

Pour the wine and sparkling water into a large pitcher. Using a vegetable peeler, peel the zest off the orange in large strips and reserve the strips. Cut the orange in half and squeeze the juice through a fine-mesh sieve into the pitcher with the wine and water. Stir together everything in the pitcher. If your wine and water aren't chilled, add 2 handfuls of ice cubes to the pitcher and give it a stir.

Fill six tall glasses halfway with ice. Put a strip of orange zest into each glass (if you don't have six strips, cut some in half; if you have more than six, just double up on some). Evenly divide the plum slices among the glasses and pour an equal amount of the wine mixture into each glass. Give each drink a stir before serving. Any leftover wine mixture can be served with more ice and plums.

Polenta + Nutella Sandwich Cookies

MAKES ABOUT 12 SANDWICH COOKIES

I never tasted Nutella until I was senior in college. That year I lived with a few friends, including my friend Katy who moved into our apartment with a supersize jar of the stuff. I got into the habit of sneaking a spoonful every night (*every single night*) and thought she would never realize it since the jar was so huge and the dips were so small. One day, overwhelmed with guilt, I decided to tell her about my indiscretion. She was, to my great surprise, *relieved* to find out that she hadn't been sleepwalking and eating it. I'll never forget the look on her face. These sandwich cookies are for her. That said, if your Nutella jar is scraped clean, these cookies are also delicious on their own as "polenta shortbread," or you can fill them with your favorite jam.

1 cup [120 g] all-purpose flour

½ cup [70 g] regular (not instant) polenta or regular cornmeal

¼ cup [50 g] sugar

½ tsp kosher salt

½ cup [110 g] cold unsalted butter, cubed

2 egg yolks

2 Tbsp water

A jar of Nutella chocolate spread

In a food processor, combine the flour, polenta, sugar, and salt and pulse to combine. Add the butter and pulse until the mixture resembles sand, about three 5-second pulses. Add the egg yolks and water and let the machine run until the mixture starts to form a single large piece of dough around the blade, about 15 seconds. Press a little of the dough between your fingers; it should hold together (similar to a pie dough). Don't be tempted to add more water or another egg yolk to make the dough smooth.

Transfer the dough to a large piece of plastic wrap and scrunch it together with your hands to form a rough log about 10 in [25 cm] long and 1¼ in [3 cm] in diameter. Wrap the dough tightly in the plastic wrap and then roll the wrapped log again so it's nice and smooth.

Place the dough in the freezer for 20 minutes or in the refrigerator for at least 1 hour or up to 48 hours. (Basically, you want to chill the dough so it's firm enough to slice, so go the freezer route if you want to make these ASAP, or use the fridge if you're making the dough ahead. If you want to make the dough up to a month ahead, you can freeze it until it is solid and then let it hang out at room temperature for about 30 minutes before slicing.)

Meanwhile, preheat your oven to 350°F [180°C]. Line a sheet pan with parchment paper.

Unwrap the dough and use a sharp chef's knife to cut the log into even slices about $\frac{1}{3}$ inch [8 mm] thick. You should have at least twenty-four slices. Evenly space the cookies on the prepared sheet pan.

Bake the cookies until golden brown around the edges, about 18 minutes. Set the pan on a wire rack and let the cookies cool for 15 minutes, then carefully transfer the cookies to the rack

and let them continue to cool to room temperature. They will become crisp as they cool.

Turn half of the cookies upside-down and spread as much Nutella on each one as you like. Place a plain cookie top, flat-side down, on each Nutella'ed cookie bottom to make sandwiches. Serve immediately or store for up to 2 days in an airtight container for a softer cookie.

It's Me Again

ARUGULA + LEMON PESTO

Put whatever dressed arugula salad is left over into a food processor along with a minced garlic clove and pulse until well combined. Add enough additional olive oil to turn the mixture into a sauce and season to taste with salt.

CREAMY SPINACH TOASTS

The spinach mixture from the baked pasta can be made on its own (or make extra on purpose) and then turned into delicious toasts. Grill, broil, or toast thick slices of bread, rub one side of each slice with a raw garlic clove to impart a little flavor, and then spread with the spinach mixture. Serve as is or run under the broiler to melt the cheese and brown the topping a little.

GARLIC TOAST MEATBALLS

Leftover Garlic + Anchovy Butter Toasts can be the foundation for meatballs. Fincly chop the toasts, put into a bowl, and add enough whole milk to moisten the bread. Let the

bread sit in the milk for a few minutes to really soften and then, for every large handful of chopped toasts, add a beaten egg, an extra handful of chopped parsley, and 1 lb [455 g] ground meat (beef, turkey, pork, or chicken work well here). Form into meatballs and roast on a half sheet pan at 425°F [220°C] until firm to the touch, about 25 minutes, depending on the size of the meatballs. Serve warm on their own or in a pot of warm tomato sauce.

JUST A NOTE

I have not included a leftover suggestion for the baked pasta. That's because I think the best thing about leftover baked pasta is not transforming it, but eating it cold out of the refrigerator. You could throw a serving in a waffle maker to warm it up and to create the most unbelievably crispy edges ever. But I recommend that only if you have a waffle maker with plates that can go in the dishwasher, or you'll be trying to clean them up forever (I learned that the hard way).

Card Night Enchiladas

———

GARLICKY SHRIMP WITH TEQUILA + LIME

CHICKEN + ROASTED TOMATO ENCHILADAS

KALE SALAD WITH PEPITA DRESSING

TOASTED COCONUT CAKE

A number of years ago, three of my closest friends and I started a ritual we eventually came to call "card night." It started when we all lived in New York City and would meet once a month at a different restaurant. That quickly became an expensive habit, and since we all love to cook, we decided to start hosting the dinners at home, rotating the get-together among our apartments. Our rule was that we wouldn't leave dinner until we had set a date for the next one. Switching to home-cooked meals made the monthly dinners more relaxed and affordable, and also more meaningful. It became a tangible way for all of us to really take care of one another. We started playing cards after we ate, letting our evenings stretch after dinner.

These monthly get-togethers lasted regularly through our late twenties and into our early thirties, and we still do them, though far less frequently now because moves upstate, marriages, and children have entered our lives. We've talked about everything during these meals, and they've really been our safe place to navigate becoming adults together. Cleo, Amelia, and Lizzy, this one is for you.

UP TO 1 MONTH AHEAD	Make the enchiladas up to the point of baking them, cover tightly with plastic wrap, and store in the freezer. Defrost in the refrigerator overnight before baking.
UP TO 3 DAYS AHEAD	Make the salad dressing and transfer to a tightly capped jar. Wash the kale and place in a plastic bag with a paper towel to absorb excess moisture. Store the dressing and kale in the fridge.
UP TO 1 DAY AHEAD	If you have not made and frozen the enchiladas, make them now up until the point of baking them, then cover tightly and refrigerate. Make the cake (don't top it yet), wrap it in plastic wrap, and store in the fridge, and then bring it to room temperature before serving.
UP TO A FEW HOURS AHEAD	Dress the salad and store it at room temperature with a damp paper towel on top. Whip the cream for the cake and keep it in a covered bowl in the refrigerator (you might need to give it an extra whisking right before serving).
LAST MOMENT	Make the shrimp when you pop the enchiladas in the oven. Enjoy the shrimp with drinks, move on to dinner, and then top the cake with cream and coconut just before serving.

Garlicky Shrimp with Tequila + Lime

SERVES 4

These shrimp are directly inspired by a card night tradition: whenever our group gets together, fresh limes and a bottle of tequila for margaritas are always on hand. I figured why not splash a little of both on some garlicky shrimp? Although I make these as a nosh with said margaritas, they could also easily be dinner. Serve them with rice and black beans, maybe with a little diced avocado on top. They would be great on top of or next to the Super Crunchy Lime-y Salad on page 227, as well. If you're not into booze, these are equally good without the tequila. Or if you're in more of an Italian mood, substitute white wine for the tequila, lemon juice and zest for the lime, and parsley for the cilantro.

2 Tbsp olive oil

1 Tbsp unsalted butter

3 garlic cloves, minced

1 lb [455 g] large shrimp, peeled and deveined

½ tsp kosher salt

3 Tbsp silver tequila

Finely grated zest of 1 small lime

2 Tbsp fresh lime juice

A small handful of fresh cilantro leaves (a little bit of stem is fine!), roughly chopped

In a large, heavy skillet over medium-high heat, warm the olive oil and butter. Once the butter melts, add the garlic and cook, stirring, until it is sizzling and very fragrant, about 30 seconds. Add the shrimp and sprinkle them with the salt. Cook the shrimp, stirring now and then, until they turn opaque, about 1½ minutes. Pour in the tequila. Let the shrimp cook until the tequila nearly evaporates, about 1 more minute.

Turn off the heat, add the lime zest and juice, and toss well to combine. Transfer the shrimp to a serving platter (or serve straight out of the pan) and sprinkle with the cilantro. Serve immediately with toothpicks.

Chicken + Roasted Tomato Enchiladas

SERVES 4, QUITE GENEROUSLY

These enchiladas are especially wonderful for a cozy group of friends because, like all casseroles, you can assemble them early in the day or even a day before and just pop them into the oven when you're having drinks. Even though it may be tempting to skip the tortilla-frying step, please don't. Heating up the tortillas and coating them with a little oil makes them not only more pliable and easier to roll but also keeps them from falling apart once they're covered in sauce. The oil is almost like a little raincoat that protects them. If you're on a health kick, you can skip the tortillas and use blanched collard green or Swiss chard leaves as wrappers (I do that version for Grace and me sometimes). Lastly, if you are cooking these for children or anyone who can't tolerate spice, feel free to swap in a poblano chile for the jalapeño (it's much milder), or just omit the fresh chile all together.

4 garlic cloves, minced

1 tsp ground cumin

2 Tbsp olive oil

Kosher salt

1½ lb [680 g] boneless, skinless chicken breasts

One 28-oz [794-g] can whole peeled tomatoes

1 jalapeño chile, roughly chopped (discard the seeds if you like)

2 large handfuls of fresh cilantro leaves (a little bit of stem is fine!)

½ cup [120 g] sour cream

3 Tbsp canola or other neutral oil, plus more as needed

Ten 6-in [15-cm] corn tortillas

¾ cup [85 g] coarsely grated Monterey Jack cheese

½ small red onion, thinly sliced

Preheat your oven to 425°F [220°C]. Line a sheet pan with parchment paper.

In a large bowl, stir together the garlic, cumin, olive oil, and 1 tsp salt. Add the chicken breasts and coat them with the garlic mixture. Place them in an even layer on one side of the prepared sheet pan.

Pour the can of tomatoes into a sieve placed over a bowl to catch the juice. Reserve the juice. Place the drained tomatoes and the jalapeño on the other side of the sheet pan.

Roast the chicken and tomatoes until the chicken is firm to the touch and golden brown and the tomatoes are a bit concentrated, about 35 minutes. Remove the pan from the oven and leave the oven on.

Transfer the chicken to a large bowl and let it cool down a bit. Transfer the tomatoes and jalapeño to a blender or food processor and add any cooking juices from the sheet pan, the reserved tomato juice, a handful of the cilantro, the sour cream, and 1 tsp kosher salt. Process until smooth. You should have about 3 cups [720 ml] sauce.

Once the chicken is cool enough to handle, shred it into bite-size pieces directly into the bowl in which it is already sitting. If any liquid remains in the bowl from the chicken, leave it there, as it will become part of its own sauce! Add one-third (about 1 cup/240 ml) of the reserved tomato sauce and stir well to combine.

Pour another third (about 1 cup/240 ml) of the tomato sauce in the bottom of a 9-by-13-in [23-by-33-cm] baking dish. Spread the sauce to cover the bottom.

In a large nonstick skillet over high heat, warm the canola oil. Place a tortilla in the pan and fry until coated with oil on both sides and just barely softened and pliable, about 10 seconds per side. Repeat with the remaining tortillas, transferring them to a work surface as you go. As long as your skillet is nonstick and nice and hot, you shouldn't need more oil, but if the skillet goes dry before you are done with the tortillas, add a splash more.

Divide the sauced chicken evenly among the tortillas. Roll up the tortillas tightly around the chicken and line them up, seam-side down, in the baking dish. Pour the remaining tomato sauce (about 1 cup/240 ml) evenly over the stuffed tortillas and sprinkle with the cheese.

Bake the enchiladas until the cheese is melted and golden brown and the sauce is bubbling, about 20 minutes. Sprinkle with the remaining handful of cilantro and the red onion and serve immediately.

Kale Salad with Pepita Dressing

SERVES 4

Pepitas, or pumpkin seeds, are a versatile ingredient. They add crunch wherever they land, and they can be transformed into an incredibly rich and creamy dressing when puréed with some liquid. Combined with garlic, cumin, and lime, they turn into an almost Mexican-inspired Caesar dressing (and a totally vegan dressing to boot). You could make the dressing in a blender, but you'll need to double or triple the batch so there's enough liquid for the blender to get going (this amount, which suits the amount of kale, doesn't move much in my blender). I love this kale salad for the same reason I love all salads made with super-hearty greens: it doesn't wilt. You can make it before dinner and it will be totally fine even if it sits for a bit. I even like it the next day. For a substantial meal on its own, mix some cooked quinoa into the salad and top with roasted chicken or grilled salmon (this idea comes from my friend Steph who tried out this recipe for me . . . thanks Steph!).

¼ cup [35 g] pumpkin seeds, lightly toasted (see Note)

1 small garlic clove, minced

½ tsp ground cumin

2 Tbsp olive oil

3 Tbsp fresh lime juice

1 tsp kosher salt

2 Tbsp water

¾ lb [340 g] curly or Lacinato kale (about 1 average bunch), tough stems discarded, finely chopped or thinly sliced

1 large watermelon radish or 4 regular radishes, trimmed and cut into matchsticks or thinly sliced

3 oz [85 g] queso fresco or feta cheese, crumbled

In a food processor, combine the pumpkin seeds, garlic, and cumin and process until finely ground. Add the olive oil, 2 Tbsp of the lime juice, ½ tsp of the salt, and the water and purée until smooth.

Put the kale into a large serving bowl, drizzle with the remaining 1 Tbsp lime juice, and sprinkle with the remaining ½ tsp salt. Use your hands to massage the lime and salt into the kale to soften it.

Drizzle three-fourths of the dressing on the kale and stir well to combine (I use my hands for this). Top the salad with the radish and cheese. Drizzle with the remaining dressing and serve immediately.

Note: To toast the pumpkin seeds, put them into a dry skillet over medium heat and cook, stirring, until they're golden brown, about 2 minutes.

Toasted Coconut Cake

SERVES 8

If I had to choose one type of cake to eat for the rest of my life, coconut cake would be my no-hesitation answer. At my bat mitzvah, I had thirteen angel food cakes topped with clouds of whipped cream and tons of grated coconut, and when Grace and I had our tiny wedding, our friend Cleo made Ina Garten's coconut layer cake for us. This version is my latest go-to. The cake is almost like a pound cake that bumped into an angel food cake, thanks to lots of whipped egg whites. I put tons of toasted coconut both in and on top of the cake and use just the slightest whisper of almond extract in the batter to boost the nutty flavor. When you make the cake, I know it might be tempting to add the sugar all in one go with the butter, but adding a little to the egg whites helps stabilize them. This is important because stabilized egg whites hold onto their air, making the cake nice and fluffy.

1½ cups [110 g] unsweetened flaked dried coconut

1½ cups [180 g] all-purpose flour

1 tsp baking powder

½ tsp kosher salt

4 egg whites

½ tsp fresh lemon juice (or distilled white or apple cider vinegar)

2 Tbsp, plus ½ cup [100 g] granulated sugar

¾ cup [165 g] unsalted butter, at room temperature

1 tsp vanilla extract

¼ tsp almond extract

½ cup [120 ml] whole milk

½ cup [120 ml] heavy cream

1 Tbsp powdered sugar

Preheat your oven to 350°F [180°C]. Spray the bottom and sides of an 8-in [20-cm] round cake pan with baking spray and line the bottom with a circle of parchment paper. Spray the parchment paper for good measure and set the pan aside.

Spread the coconut on a sheet pan and bake, stirring now and then, until light golden brown, about 5 minutes. Set the coconut aside to cool.

In a large bowl, whisk together the flour, baking powder, and salt. Put the egg whites into a stand mixer fitted with the whisk attachment (or use a handheld electric mixer or a whisk and some elbow grease) and beat on medium-high speed until foamy, about 30 seconds. With the mixer still running on medium-high speed, slowly add the lemon juice and 2 Tbsp of the granulated sugar and continue beating until the egg whites billow and turn into a white, fluffy, almost glossy cloud of stiff peaks, about another 2 minutes. To test if the egg whites are stiff enough, lift the whisk attachment. The whites that cling to it should stand nice and tall and not droop over (that's a soft peak). If they're not quite there yet, just keep mixing until they are. Transfer the egg whites to a separate bowl and hang on to them (if using a handheld electric mixer or whisk, just set the bowl with the egg whites aside).

(Continued)

47

Put the butter, the remaining ½ cup [100 g] granulated sugar, and the vanilla and almond extracts into the same bowl you just used for beating the egg whites (no need to wash it). (If using a handheld electric mixer or whisk, use a clean bowl.) Beat on medium-high speed, stopping to scrape down the sides of the bowl, until light and fluffy, about 1½ minutes. Add half of the milk and mix on low speed until well combined, then add half of the flour mixture and continue to mix on low speed until well combined. Repeat to incorporate the remaining milk and flour.

Use a rubber spatula to fold one-third of the beaten egg whites into the cake batter. It's okay if you sort of stir this one-third in rather than fold it in, as the cake batter is quite stiff and these egg whites will help lighten it. Add another third of the egg whites and gently and carefully fold them into the batter by cutting your spatula down through the middle of the bowl, scraping the bottom of the bowl, and then pulling the mixture back up. Think of it like cutting in the egg whites and folding them with the batter. This helps preserve the air you worked hard to create in the egg whites. Fold in the rest of the egg whites and then gently fold in ¾ cup [55 g] of the toasted coconut. Use the rubber spatula to scrape the batter into the prepared pan and then to smooth the surface so it is even.

Bake the cake until golden brown, firm to the touch, and a toothpick inserted in the center comes out relatively clean without wet crumbs stuck to it, about 35 minutes. Set the cake pan on a wire rack and let the cake cool to room temperature.

Combine the cream and powdered sugar in the stand mixer and beat on medium-high speed until soft peaks form, about 2 minutes (or use a bowl and a whisk and some solid effort).

Use a dinner knife to loosen the edges of the cake from the pan sides and then invert it onto your work surface. Peel off and discard the parchment, then invert the cake one more time onto a serving platter. If a few crumbs come loose and you eat them, I won't tell. Spoon the soft whipped cream on top of the cake. Sprinkle the cream with the remaining toasted coconut.

Cut into wedges and serve. Leftovers can be covered and stored in the refrigerator for up to 2 days.

It's Me Again

SHRIMP + KIMCHI PANCAKES

Whisk together 2 eggs with ½ cup [70 g] white rice flour or ½ cup [60 g] all-purpose flour and a large pinch of salt. Stir in up to a large handful of chopped leftover shrimp and another handful of chopped cabbage kimchi. Fry the pancakes in a hot nonstick skillet slicked with a little canola oil until browned and crisp on both sides. I like to make these on the small side—the size of a silver dollar—so they're easier to handle and you get crispier edges. Mix together equal parts mayonnaise and juice from the kimchi jar to use for dipping.

CREAMY ROASTED TOMATO SOUP

Purposely make a double batch of the sauce for the enchiladas. Use half for the enchiladas and add 3 cups [720 ml] vegetable or chicken stock to the rest, and that's that. So delicious, and two meals for the price of one. Serve with quesadillas instead of grilled cheese sandwiches.

CALDO GALLEGO

Leftover kale salad can also be transformed into *caldo gallego*, the traditional soup from Galicia, Spain. Sauté a chopped onion and a handful of chopped cured Spanish chorizo in a little olive oil. Once soft, add 8 cups [2 L] chicken stock and two diced potatoes. Once the potatoes are soft, add the leftover kale salad. Serve hot.

KALE KUKU SABZI

Leftover kale salad can be turned into a version of *kuku sabzi*, the great Persian herb frittata. Start by softening a finely chopped washed leek in a little olive oil in a medium broiler-safe nonstick skillet. Beat together 4 eggs and 1 tsp *each* salt, baking powder, and ground turmeric. Finely chop whatever kale salad remains (it's okay if it's dressed and if a little cheese ends up in the eggs, but avoid the radishes) and add it to the eggs along with the softened leek and 2 large handfuls each finely chopped fresh cilantro, Italian parsley, and dill. The mixture should be more like kale and herbs mixed with eggs than the other way around. Add a glug of oil to the skillet you cooked the leek in and set it over medium heat. Add the egg mixture to the skillet and cook until the bottom is set, about 8 minutes. Place the skillet under the broiler and cook the frittata just until the top is set and the whole thing is barely firm to the touch, about 2 minutes. Serve warm or at room temperature, cut into wedges.

Rosh Hashanah Dinner

CELEBRATION CHICKEN WITH SWEET POTATOES + DATES

BAKED SAFFRON RICE

BEET SALAD WITH POPPY SEED + CHIVE DRESSING

APPLESAUCE CAKE WITH CREAM CHEESE + HONEY FROSTING

My mother has always described herself as a "gastronomic Jew." While I don't consider myself religious, I can get behind that label. For my entire life, Jewish holidays have provided wonderful memories, all accompanied by some of my favorite foods. When I think about my family, I think of long tables piled with things like gefilte fish and matzo ball soup, honey cake and coconut macaroons. I think of running through my Uncle Jeff and Aunt Sharon's house with my band of cousins looking for the *afikoman* (the symbolic piece of matzo that's hidden during the Passover meal). Lately I have been thinking about all of the additions to our family table, like my wife and sister-in-law and my cousins' spouses and all of the babies and dogs that come with these new marriages. The holidays also give us all a moment to remember the folks who used to be with us.

As a cook, I've come to love the reliable repetition of holiday foods and the comforting way it feels to expect the same dishes every year. Because I am someone who is constantly coming up with new recipes, purposefully repeating a menu and letting familiar dishes reappear is totally relaxing. I especially love making dishes for my family with symbolic ingredients that we've all eaten for generations, which imbues them with so much meaning. This menu provides plenty of food for eight or so people. Feel free to cut everything in half or, if you've got a family as large as mine, feel free to double or even triple the amounts.

UP TO 3 DAYS AHEAD	Mix everything for the chicken and store in a resealable plastic bag in the refrigerator. Make the rice, cook and slice the beets, and make the dressing for the beets, then store all of these things in separate containers in the refrigerator.
UP TO 1 DAY AHEAD	Bake the cake, wrap in plastic wrap, and store at room temperature.
UP TO A FEW HOURS AHEAD	Bring the cream cheese for the cake frosting to room temperature, make the frosting, and frost the cake.
UP TO 1 HOUR AHEAD	Pop the chicken in the oven. A little while after it goes in, cook or warm the rice in the oven.
LAST MOMENT	Dress the beets.

Celebration Chicken with Sweet Potatoes + Dates

SERVES 8 TO 10

Rosh Hashanah celebrates the Jewish New Year. There are a lot of symbolic foods associated with the holiday, most of them sweet to help usher in a sweet new year. This chicken is a bit of a Rosh Hashanah riff on the famous Chicken Marbella from the *The Silver Palate Cookbook* by Sheila Lukins and Julee Rosso. Just like that extremely popular recipe, this chicken doesn't require much work and yields a crowd-pleasing, highly flavorful result. It calls for just one roasting pan, in which you both mix everything and cook. There are no extra bowls or pans, no browning chicken in batches, and definitely no fuss. You also get a two-for-one moment: the sweet potatoes and dates (sweet for Rosh Hashanah!) give you an instant side dish.

¼ cup [60 ml] apple cider vinegar

¼ cup [60 ml] olive oil

¼ cup [60 ml] water

8 garlic cloves, minced

1 Tbsp kosher salt

2 tsp freshly ground black pepper

Two 3- to 4-lb [1.4- to 1.8-kg] chickens, each cut into 10 pieces (2 wings, 2 legs, 2 thighs, and 2 breasts cut in half across the bone), backbone discarded (or saved for another use, like stock), at room temperature

3 large sweet potatoes, about 2 lb [910 g] total, unpeeled, scrubbed and cut into bite-size pieces

12 large dried dates (preferably Medjool), halved and pitted

A small handful of chopped fresh soft herbs (cilantro, parsley, dill, and/or chives all work well)

Preheat your oven to 425°F [220°C].

In a large roasting pan, whisk together the vinegar, olive oil, water, garlic, salt, and pepper (you want a pan that's big enough to hold all of the chicken pieces in a single layer; a disposable aluminum pan is good for this if your roasting pan isn't large enough). Add the chicken pieces, sweet potatoes, and dates. Use your hands to mix everything together and get the marinade on all of chicken, sweet potatoes, and dates. Warning: the following is a bit messy, but bear with me. Move everything around so the sweet potatoes and dates are in a single layer on the bottom of the pan and the chicken pieces, skin-side up, are in a single, even layer on top.

Roast until the sweet potatoes are tender (test with a fork or a paring knife) and the chicken pieces are firm to the touch and their exposed skin is nicely browned, about 1 hour. Let the chicken rest at room temperature for at least 15 minutes before serving.

To serve, transfer the chicken, sweet potatoes, and dates to a large serving platter and pour all of the cooking juices over the top (or serve directly from the roasting pan, giving everything a little mix first). Sprinkle with the herbs and serve warm.

Baked Saffron Rice

SERVES 8 TO 10

Inspired by a Yotam Ottolenghi recipe, this rice is great because it feeds a lot of people, it's foolproof since you cook it in the oven (which helps rice cook so much more evenly than it does on the stove top, leaving the cook calm), and you can prepare it ahead and reheat it before serving. The saffron makes it very aromatic and special (perfect for a holiday). It's an expensive ingredient, but a little bit goes a very long way. Incidentally, the rice is delicious with or without it, and you can also add different spices when you cook the garlic and onion (whole or ground cloves, cardamom pods, and cinnamon sticks are all welcome).

½ cup [120 ml] olive oil

6 garlic cloves, minced

1 medium yellow onion, finely diced

2½ cups [500 g] long-grain white rice (preferably basmati)

1 Tbsp kosher salt, plus more as needed

4 cups [960 ml] plus 3 Tbsp boiling water

3 large pinches of saffron threads

Preheat your oven to 425°F [220°C].

In a large, heavy, oven-safe pot over medium-low heat, warm the olive oil. Add the garlic and onion and cook, stirring now and then, until the vegetables sizzle and soften, about 8 minutes. Turn off the heat and add the rice and salt and stir everything together.

Pour in 4 cups [960 ml] of the boiling water and stir well to combine. Cover the pot tightly and place in the oven. Bake until the liquid is absorbed and the rice is cooked through, about 25 minutes (the center of the rice might be cooked less than the rice around it, but it will rest in just a moment and all of the grains will turn out tender . . . trust me).

While the rice is cooking, put the saffron into a small bowl and add the remaining 3 Tbsp boiling water.

When the rice is ready, uncover it and spoon the reserved saffron and its liquid evenly over the top. Re-cover the pot and let the rice sit for at least 15 minutes and up to 1 hour before serving.

Uncover the rice, fluff with a fork or a spoon, and stir well to incorporate the saffron. Taste and season with more salt if needed. Serve warm. If you want to cook the rice more than an hour ahead of serving, rewarm it in the pot in a 250°F [120°C] oven, stirring now and then, until heated through, about 15 minutes from room temperature or 30 minutes if cold from the refrigerator.

Beet Salad
with Poppy Seed + Chive Dressing

SERVES 8 TO 10

I always like making unfussy vegetable dishes as part of more elaborate holiday menus. They add color and variety to your spread, and you can also rest assured your guests can fill their plates with something healthy. This beet salad is one of my go-to vegetable dishes because it's a little unexpected yet totally easy to make, and you can whip up the dressing and cook and slice the beets ahead of time and easily assemble the whole thing at the last minute. Also, it's best served barely warm or at room temperature, which makes it especially perfect for a big dinner.

If you can't find poppy seeds, just leave them out. The beet salad will be just as good without them. I like adding them because I love how they look and I also love the little crunch they add, plus I think of them as a nod to poppy seed bagels, which were an integral part of my gastronomic-Jewish upbringing.

Kosher salt

2½ lbs [1.2 kg] red beets, scrubbed

2 Tbsp plain yogurt or mayonnaise

2 Tbsp olive oil

2 tsp Dijon mustard

2½ Tbsp apple cider vinegar

¼ tsp freshly ground black pepper

1½ Tbsp poppy seeds

3 Tbsp minced fresh chives (or a thinly sliced scallion minus the tough ends)

Bring a large saucepan of salted water to a boil and add the beets (the water should cover the beets; if it doesn't, add more). Cook the beets, turning them every so often, until they're tender (test with a paring knife), about 45 minutes (it may be a bit less or a bit longer depending on the size and age of the beets, so start testing at 30 minutes).

Drain the beets, transfer to a paper towel–lined cutting board, and use the paper towels to rub off the skins. Trim off and discard the root ends.

Meanwhile, in a small bowl, whisk together the yogurt, olive oil, mustard, vinegar, pepper, poppy seeds, 2 Tbsp of the chives, and ½ tsp salt.

Slice the warm beets into thin bite-size wedges or thin rounds (whatever you prefer) and transfer them to a large serving bowl or platter. Season them lightly with salt and then drizzle the dressing evenly over them. Sprinkle with the remaining 1 Tbsp chives. Serve immediately.

Applesauce Cake with Cream Cheese + Honey Frosting

SERVES 8 TO 10

The food most closely associated with Rosh Hashanah is apples dipped in honey, an autumnal gesture to shepherd in a sweet year. A lot of desserts feature apples and honey, and this super-simple cake (which requires one bowl and one cake pan) fills the bill. I like this cake so much (and especially love how easy it is to make) that I make it often, especially throughout the fall when apples are on the mind. Its texture and appeal are similar to those of banana bread. If you like, you can stir in a large handful or two of raisins and/or nuts just before you scrape the batter into the cake pan. Although you can absolutely use homemade applesauce for this, know that store-bought is just fine.

CAKE

2 cups [240 g] all-purpose flour

1 Tbsp ground cinnamon

1 Tbsp ground ginger

1½ tsp kosher salt

2 tsp baking soda

2 eggs, beaten

½ cup [100 g] sugar

½ cup [120 ml] buttermilk or [120 g] plain yogurt

1½ cups [400 g] unsweetened applesauce

⅓ cup [80 ml] canola or other neutral oil

FROSTING

6 oz [170 g] cream cheese, at room temperature

2 Tbsp sour cream

¼ cup [85 g] honey

Pinch of kosher salt

To make the cake: Preheat your oven to 350°F [180°C]. Spray the bottom and sides of a 9-in [23-cm] round cake pan with baking spray and line the bottom with a circle of parchment paper. Set the pan aside.

In a large bowl, whisk together the flour, cinnamon, ginger, salt, and baking soda. Add the eggs, sugar, buttermilk, applesauce, and oil and whisk gently just until everything is combined. Use a rubber spatula to scrape the batter into the prepared pan and then smooth the surface so it is even.

Bake the cake until it is just barely firm to the touch and a toothpick inserted in the center comes out clean, about 55 minutes. Set the cake aside on a wire rack to cool to room temperature.

Use a dinner knife to loosen the edges of the cake from the pan sides and then invert it onto your work surface. Peel off and discard the parchment. Invert the cake one more time onto a serving platter.

(Continued)

To make the frosting: In a large bowl, combine the cream cheese, sour cream, honey, and salt and whisk together aggressively until the cream cheese is slightly aerated (you can also do this with a handheld electric mixer or in a stand mixer).

Spread the frosting over the top of the cake and don't worry too much about making this perfect. I think a not-too-perfect cake is so much better than a perfect cake. Cut into wedges and serve. Leftovers can be wrapped in plastic wrap and stored in the refrigerator for up to 3 days.

It's Me Again

CORONATION CHICKEN SALAD

Shred whatever chicken you have left (discard the skin and bones) and roughly chop the leftover sweet potatoes and dates. Put all of that into a bowl, sprinkle with a generous amount of curry powder, and add a large spoonful of mango chutney (or apricot jam, or just leave it out if you've got enough sweet dates) and stir to mix. Add just enough mayonnaise (or plain Greek yogurt) to bind everything together and season to taste with salt and pepper. Fold in some thinly sliced scallions and, if you'd like a bit of crunch, some chopped roasted almonds. Serve on toast or in lettuce cups.

STUFFED PEPPERS

This is for your leftover rice. Halve bell peppers lengthwise and remove the seeds and ribs (you can leave the stems on if you like, as they're attractive). Arrange them, hollow-side up, in a single layer in a roasting pan. Mix whatever leftover rice you have with a generous amount of crumbled feta cheese and some chopped fresh herbs (a lot of Italian parsley is simple and nice). Fill the pepper halves with the rice and dot the tops with butter and/ or drizzle with olive oil. Add about ½ cup [120 ml] water or chicken stock to the roasting pan and place in a 350°F [180°C] oven. Roast until the peppers are soft and the top of the rice is a little bit browned, about 25 minutes.

Serve warm or at room temperature. These are especially good topped with a dollop of plain yogurt. If you don't want the peppers to be vegetarian, you can add some crumbled cooked sausage meat or ground meat (beef, turkey, and lamb all work well) to the rice mixture before filling the peppers.

BEET DIP

As simple as can be, put leftover beet salad with its dressing into a food processor and pulse until puréed. You can make the dip as smooth or as rustic as you like. Season it to taste with salt and pepper and add a splash of vinegar or a squeeze of lemon juice if you need a little extra edge. Serve with crackers, toasted bread, or carrots or on endive leaves or cucumber slices . . . anything!

CHEESY RICE FRITTERS

For every large handful of leftover rice, mix together with a handful of grated Cheddar cheese, a beaten egg, and 2 Tbsp of all-purpose flour. Cook spoonfuls in a lightly oiled skillet until browned and crisp on both sides. Sprinkle with salt and serve hot. These are great with drinks or topped with eggs for breakfast (almost like hash browns).

No Stress Thanksgiving

———————

ROAST TURKEY BREAST + ONIONS WITH MUSTARD + SAGE

APPLE CIDER GRAVY

SHEET PAN BREAD STUFFING WITH SAUSAGE + SPINACH

RADICCHIO + ROASTED SQUASH SALAD

STRING BEANS WITH TOASTED ALMONDS + LEMON

MAPLE ROASTED APPLES WITH VANILLA ICE CREAM + ROASTED PECANS

EASY PUMPKIN + OLIVE OIL CAKE

When it comes to Thanksgiving, my newest tradition, which is way more important than any recipe, is to look into organizations like Women Empowering Women for Indian Nations (WEWIN) and the American Indian College Fund and donate if you have the means, or at least spread the word. While Thanksgiving brings up a lot of positive memories for many of us, it's also a symbol of some of the hard truths about American history. Also check out Give Back + Do Good (see page 288) for more ways to help folks who might not have easy access to a large meal with family and friends.

Being able to hold the good with the tough means having a clearer understanding of the meaning of Thanksgiving. Personally, it also allows me to more deeply embrace the opportunity to gather a group of diverse family members and friends in my home.

(Continued)

MONDAY (3 DAYS AHEAD)

Buy all of your groceries and put them away (a feat for this holiday!) and you can make the gravy (it feels great to cross something off of the list on Monday). Also call everyone you assigned things to and make sure they're on top of their duties.

TUESDAY (2 DAYS AHEAD)

Tear the bread for the stuffing and leave it out to dry. Chop the onions and celery for the stuffing (stash in a plastic bag), parboil the string beans, shred the radicchio for the salad (put into a plastic bag with an ever-so-damp paper towel), roast the squash for the salad, make the salad dressing, and store all of these in the refrigerator. Make the cake (it holds well for days!) and wrap in plastic and store at room temperature.

WEDNESDAY (1 DAY AHEAD)

Roast the apples, finish the stuffing up to the point of baking it, and season the turkey breast. Store in a plastic bag in the refrigerator. You could assemble the salad if you want, or wait until tomorrow.

THURSDAY (DAY OF)

Roast the turkey breast, warm the gravy in a pot, bake the stuffing, finish the string beans in a skillet, and assemble the salad if you haven't already. While you're eating, warm the apples in the now-empty oven and take out the ice cream while dishes are being gathered so that it's at that perfect easy-to-scoop moment when it's time for dessert. Slice the cake. Put your feet up.

If you are cooking Thanksgiving for a big group like I have since I was about eleven (where was *Chopped Junior* in the 1990s?), here are some things that are helpful to keep in mind.

• Do you tend to make a similar meal each year like I do? Then when you write your menu and grocery list this year, make a copy of it (mine is starred in my email archives) and use it again and again. Even if you switch up a few dishes, you can just edit the list, not start it from scratch.

• The hardest part of any meal isn't preparing any single dish. It's nailing the timing. The best way to handle this? Don't be afraid to choose things that are great at room temperature! Side

dishes are especially forgiving (like the string beans and roasted squash salad). Serving them at room temperature means they can be prepared ahead and just left out, making them one less thing to worry about.

• Just about every dish has some part of it that can be prepared ahead of time. Don't start cooking on Thursday morning. Start as soon as Monday! Tear bread for stuffing and let it get dry and kind of stale so it will absorb everything you add to it. Parboil string beans and put them into a plastic bag, and then at the last minute, heat them up in a big skillet with oil and garlic. Make salad dressing and put it into a jar. And on and on.

• When people ask what they can bring, tell them. I always delegate wine, pies, cranberry sauce (my grandma makes the best, and I'm not going to mess with that), and a bag of ice. You can also assign things like side dishes or even the turkey if you wish. You don't have to be a hero. In fact, you'll be happier if you don't try to be one and everyone else will be more relaxed, too. Trust me, no one will remember if you made your own pie crust or even your own pie.

• If you are a guest, bring something, and when you walk in the door, ask what you can do. Even if your host tells you not to bring something, bring something. It could even be breakfast for Friday morning (see page 276 for lots of ideas).

• Every year my in-laws arrive on Wednesday, and when my mother-in-law asks what she can bring, I ask her to prepare something we can all eat Wednesday night. I love this tradition. Even if your mother-in-law doesn't show up with meatballs from your first cookbook (tear inducing!), go out to dinner on Wednesday night or order takeout.

Roast Turkey Breast + Onions with Mustard + Sage

SERVES 12

I often make one small whole turkey and an extra turkey breast for my Thanksgiving. Most of the crowd at my house prefers white meat, and I really like it left over for sandwiches, so this plan makes the most sense for our holiday. This is my go-to recipe for turkey breast that is the opposite of dry and boring and also cooks *so quickly*, which is the antithesis of most Thanksgiving turkey. The real trick here is getting boneless, skin-on turkey breasts, which you essentially treat as really large boneless chicken breasts. To serve twelve, you'll need more than one turkey breast. If you don't have a roasting pan large enough to roast the turkey breasts in a single layer, use two pans (double the onions, oil, and water and rotate the pans halfway through roasting).

½ cup [120 g] Dijon mustard

2 Tbsp kosher salt

1 Tbsp freshly ground black pepper

1 large bunch fresh sage

6 lb [2.7 kg] boneless, skin-on turkey breast halves, at room temperature, patted dry with paper towels (see Note)

2 large yellow onions, thickly sliced (as if you were making onion rings)

2 Tbsp olive oil

¾ cup [180 ml] water

Preheat your oven to 425°F [220°C].

In a small bowl, stir together the mustard, salt, and pepper. Pick 12 sage leaves from their stems (reserve the stems and the remaining sage), mince them, add them to the mustard mixture, and mix well. Rub the mixture all over the turkey breasts. If you have time, it's nice to let the meat sit at room temperature for an hour with the seasonings before roasting (or up to overnight in the refrigerator, but bring it back to room temperature before roasting).

Place the onions on the bottom of a roasting pan large enough to hold the turkey breasts comfortably in a single layer. Drizzle with the olive oil and arrange the remaining sage (including the stems from the leaves you minced) over the onions. Place the turkey breasts, skin-side up, on top of the onions. Pour the water into the pan, being careful not to pour it directly on the turkey.

Roast the turkey until the skin is golden brown, about 30 minutes. Turn the oven down to 350°F [180°C] and continue to roast until the turkey is firm to the touch and an instant-read thermometer inserted in the thickest part of each breast registers 165°F [75°C], 25 to 35 more minutes, depending on the thickness.

Transfer the turkey breasts to a cutting board and let them rest for at least 15 minutes. Remove and discard the sage leaves from the roasting pan and transfer the onions to a serving platter, preferably a warmed one.

Transfer the pan juices to your gravy (see page 70) and let them simmer and make the gravy even better than it already is. Alternatively, if you're not making gravy, keep the pan juices for serving.

Once rested, slice the turkey as thinly or thickly as you like. Place the slices on top of the onions and drizzle with the gravy or pan juices. Serve warm.

Note: If you can find only bone-in turkey breasts, either have your butcher take them off the bone or do it yourself (it's not as hard as it seems; just get a sharp knife and follow the bones) and use the bones for stock for your gravy. If you buy turkey breasts on the bone, note that they should weigh more (add about 2 lb/910 g to the total weight). If your turkey breasts come tied like a roast or in netting, remove all of that and just keep them nice and flat (this way they will cook more quickly and are less likely to dry out).

Apple Cider Gravy

MAKES ABOUT 4 CUPS [960 ML], ENOUGH FOR 12 GENEROUS SERVINGS

For the record, gravy doesn't need to be made last minute. I think it's an anxiety-inducing myth that has made many people scared of hosting Thanksgiving. Make it ahead! This is a relatively thin gravy, which is how I've always preferred it. If you like superthick gravy, simply double the flour.

½ cup [110 g] unsalted
butter, cubed

1 medium yellow onion,
finely diced

2 garlic cloves, minced

1 Tbsp minced fresh sage

1½ tsp kosher salt, plus more
as needed

1 tsp freshly ground
black pepper, plus more as
needed

¼ cup [30 g] all-purpose flour

2 cups [480 ml] chicken stock
(or turkey stock made from
the neck and other parts)

2 cups [480 ml] apple cider

In a medium saucepan over medium heat, melt the butter. Add the onion, garlic, sage, salt, and pepper and cook, stirring now and then, until the aromatics are just softened but not browned, about 8 minutes. Add the flour and stir well to combine. Let the mixture cook, stirring quite a bit, until it turns the color of a milky cup of coffee, a solid 5 minutes. While whisking constantly, slowly pour in the stock and the cider. It will seem very loose at first but trust in the power of flour. Bring the mixture just to a boil and then lower the heat and simmer, stirring now and then, until thickened and the flavor is nice and rich, about 10 minutes.

You can keep the gravy warm over the lowest heat for up to an hour, or you can make it ahead, refrigerate it, and then just warm it over low heat. You can also add drippings from your roasted turkey and/or roasted turkey breast and let the gravy reduce until it's the consistency you like. Taste and adjust the seasoning with salt and pepper before serving. For a more refined, smooth gravy, strain it through a fine-mesh sieve before serving (I don't ever bother doing this, but then again I'm not super refined).

Sheet Pan Bread Stuffing with Sausage + Spinach

SERVES 12

Since stuffing rarely appears separate from Thanksgiving, it's an inherently nostalgic and meaningful dish. I bake my stuffing on a sheet pan so the crispy-to-soft ratio is basically one to one. If you prefer it softer, bake it in a smaller vessel like a baking dish.

1¼ lb [570 g] country bread or sourdough bread, torn into bite-size pieces (about 9 cups)

2 Tbsp olive oil

1 lb [455 g] Italian fennel sausages, casings removed

2 yellow onions, diced

4 celery stalks, diced

6 garlic cloves, minced

Kosher salt

12 large fresh sage leaves, tough stems discarded, minced

1½ cups [360 ml] chicken or turkey stock

One 10-oz [280-g] package frozen spinach, defrosted, squeezed dry, and roughly chopped

2 large handfuls of fresh Italian parsley leaves (a little bit of stem is fine!), finely chopped

3 eggs

2 Tbsp unsalted butter, finely diced

Preheat your oven to 400°F [200°C].

Spread the bread cubes on a sheet pan and toast, stirring now and then, until lightly browned and crisp, about 10 minutes. Set the bread aside to cool. You can skip this step if you use stale bread.

Meanwhile, put the olive oil into a large pot over medium-high heat. Crumble in the sausage and cook, stirring now and then, until all of the fat is rendered and the meat is crisp and browned, about 15 minutes. Add the onions, celery, garlic, and 1 tsp salt to the pot and turn down the heat to medium. Cook the vegetables, stirring now and then, until slightly softened, about 10 minutes. Add the sage and stock and turn the heat to high. Once it is at a boil, turn off the heat. Stir in the spinach, parsley, and reserved bread. Taste the mixture and season with salt if more is needed. Add the eggs and give everything one good final stir.

Line the sheet pan you toasted the bread on with parchment paper. Transfer the stuffing mixture to the pan and spread it out in an even layer. Dot the top with the butter. Bake until the top is browned and the edges are nice and crispy, about 25 minutes. Serve hot.

Radicchio + Roasted Squash Salad

SERVES 12

This salad is especially great for the holiday not only for its wonderful fall flavors but also because it's hearty and can sit on a buffet table for hours without losing any integrity or flavor. In fact, you can mix the whole thing up to a day before, refrigerate it, and then bring it to room temperature before serving. If you can find delicata squash, try it (just seed it, no need to peel it). Note that if you can't find squash (or if you dislike it), sweet potatoes make an excellent substitute.

3 lb [1.3 kg] butternut squash, halved lengthwise, tough skin peeled and ends trimmed and discarded, seeded, and cut into 1-in [2.5-cm] pieces

¾ cup [180 ml] olive oil

Kosher salt

Freshly ground black pepper

2 Tbsp Dijon mustard

1 Tbsp honey or maple syrup

¼ cup [60 ml] apple cider vinegar

1 garlic clove, minced

3 heads radicchio, each about ½ lb [230 g], cored and thinly sliced

Position one rack in the center of your oven and a second rack in the top third and preheat to 400°F [200°C]. Line two sheet pans with parchment paper.

Divide the squash evenly between the prepared pans, then drizzle each pan with 2 Tbsp of the olive oil and season generously with salt and pepper. Use your hands to toss everything.

Roast the squash, stirring once or twice along the way and switching the pans between the racks and rotating them back to front halfway through the roasting, until softened and browned, about 30 minutes. Set the squash aside to cool down a bit.

In a large bowl, whisk together the mustard, honey, vinegar, and garlic. While whisking constantly, slowly drizzle in the remaining ½ cup [120 ml] olive oil to make a dressing. Season to taste with salt and pepper. Add the reserved squash and the radicchio to the bowl and use your hands to combine everything gently (messy, but fun).

Transfer the salad to a serving platter and serve immediately (or within a few hours; it holds well at room temperature).

String Beans with Toasted Almonds + Lemon

SERVES 12

A version of good old "green beans amandine," these could not be simpler to prepare. You basically parboil the beans (which can be done on Tuesday, allowing you to cross one more thing off your list!) and then heat them in garlicky oil with some crunchy almonds and bright lemon juice. This trifecta takes regular old string beans from ordinary to memorable with very little effort. They are as good warm as they are at room temperature.

Kosher salt

2 lb [910 g] string beans, topped and tailed

¼ cup [60 ml] olive oil

3 garlic cloves, minced

½ cup [70 g] unsalted roasted almonds, roughly chopped

Finely grated zest and juice of 2 lemons

Bring a large pot of water to a boil and salt it generously. Add the beans and cook, stirring, until they're bright green and just tender, about 2 minutes. Drain the beans and set aside.

Put the olive oil into the largest skillet you've got and set it over medium heat. Add the garlic and almonds and cook, stirring, until the garlic begins to sizzle, about 30 seconds. Add half of the green beans, sprinkle them with a large pinch of salt, and stir to combine with the garlicky olive oil and the almonds. Add the remaining green beans and season them with salt and give everything a good stir (this double seasoning helps to season the beans evenly, as there's a large amount of food in the pan). Cook just until the beans are warmed through, about 1 minute.

Stir in the lemon zest and juice and then transfer the beans to a serving platter. Scrape the almonds, which inevitably fall to the bottom of the skillet, over the top. Give the beans one final sprinkle of salt and serve warm or at room temperature.

Maple Roasted Apples with Vanilla Ice Cream + Roasted Pecans

SERVES 12

These apples are wonderful because they're a slightly lighter option on the Thanksgiving dessert table, which I find especially welcome after a big meal. They're also an ideal choice if you're hosting the holiday because you can roast them ahead of time and warm them just before serving (you can even warm them in their roasting pan on an outdoor grill like I did one year when I ran out of oven space). I like them for breakfast the next morning, too, either cold with yogurt or smashed into a bowl of hot oatmeal. If you have guests who can't have sugar but want something a little sweet, they even work well without the maple syrup. And if you need a vegan dessert option, olive oil or coconut oil can be used in place of the butter (and serve with nondairy ice cream). Versatility is the name of the game here.

1 cup [120 g] pecans, roughly chopped

4 Tbsp [55 g] unsalted butter, melted

¼ cup [80 g] maple syrup

1½ tsp ground cinnamon

½ tsp kosher salt

12 crisp apples (such as Honeycrisp or Granny Smith), cut into thick wedges and cored

Vanilla ice cream for serving

Preheat your oven to 400°F [200°C].

Spread the pecans on a sheet pan and roast, stirring now and then, until browned and fragrant, about 10 minutes. Set the pecans aside to cool.

In a small bowl, whisk together the butter, maple syrup, cinnamon, and salt.

Place the apples in a large roasting pan and drizzle the maple syrup mixture over them. Use your hands to coat the apples with the mixture.

Roast the apples until they've softened and browned around the edges, about 30 minutes.

Serve the apples hot, warm, or at room temperature, with the syrup from the pan drizzled over the top. Top each serving with some of the pecans and plenty of ice cream.

Easy Pumpkin + Olive Oil Cake

SERVES 12 AS A SECOND DESSERT (MORE LIKE 8 IF IT'S THE ONLY OPTION)

This not-too-sweet cake is really more like a quick bread, in the same family as zucchini and banana breads. But I like baking it in a cake pan and serving it in wedges, so I call it a cake. Call it whatever you want, just make it! It's perfect served next to the roasted apples with ice cream in this menu. If you're not making the apples, just serve the cake on its own in the afternoon with coffee or tea or as dessert with a scoop of vanilla ice cream—or better yet, with maple or butter pecan ice cream (or a dollop of whipped cream, crème fraîche, or sour cream).

2½ cups [300 g] all-purpose flour

2½ tsp baking powder

1 tsp kosher salt

1 Tbsp ground cinnamon

1 Tbsp ground ginger

2 eggs

One 15-oz [425-g] can puréed pumpkin (not pumpkin pie filling, just unsweetened puréed pumpkin)

¾ cup [180 ml] olive oil

¾ cup [150 g] packed light brown sugar

Preheat your oven to 350°F [180°C]. Spray the bottom and sides of a 9-in [23-cm] round cake pan with baking spray and line the bottom with a circle of parchment paper. Spray the parchment paper for good measure and set the pan aside.

In a large bowl, whisk together the flour, baking powder, salt, cinnamon, and ginger.

Crack the eggs into another large bowl and whisk well to combine. Add the pumpkin, olive oil, and brown sugar and whisk to mix well. Stir the flour mixture into the egg mixture until just combined. Use a rubber spatula to scrape the batter into the prepared pan and then smooth the surface so it is even.

Bake the cake until golden brown, barely firm to the touch, and a toothpick inserted in the center comes out clean, about 45 minutes. Let the cake cool in the pan on a wire rack to room temperature.

Use a dinner knife to loosen the edges of the cake from the pan sides and then invert it onto your work surface. Peel off and discard the parchment, then invert the cake one more time onto a serving platter. Cut into wedges and serve.

It's Me Again

CRISPY STUFFING WITH FRIED EGGS

Leftover stuffing makes for a decadent breakfast. Simply set a large nonstick or well-seasoned cast-iron pan over medium-high heat and warm up a slick of olive oil or butter. Add a serving of stuffing and spread it so it covers the surface. Let it cook, undisturbed, until browned and crisp on the bottom, about 2 minutes. Give the stuffing a stir and cook until completely warmed through, about 2 more minutes. Transfer to a serving plate. Fry 2 eggs in the same skillet and place them right on top of the stuffing (tip: put a few drops of water into the pan and cover the pan so the eggs steam on top). Eat immediately while everything is hot and the yolks are runny.

SHREDDED TURKEY, STRING BEANS + CUCUMBERS WITH SOY + GINGER

Leftover roast turkey and leftover string beans can be turned into a whole new thing. Discard the skin on the turkey and shred the meat into large pieces. (I prefer the texture of shredded meat here over diced, but the latter is faster, so by all means go for it if you'd like.) Put the shredded turkey into a large bowl with whatever string beans you have left (the almonds are great, too). Make a quick dressing with equal parts soy sauce, lemon juice, and olive oil and add as much peeled and minced or grated fresh ginger as you can handle (I like this to have a lot of bite, so I use quite a bit). Dress the turkey and green beans. If you like cilantro, now is the time to add some. Serve cold next to a platter of sliced cucumbers. Your turkey is now unrecognizable from Thanksgiving and is bright and crunchy and good.

ROASTED APPLESAUCE

Pass leftover roasted apples, with their syrup, through a food mill or pulse in a food processor (which will leave bits of skin in the sauce, but that's okay with me). That's it! Serve on top of oatmeal or with yogurt or just on its own for a great snack.

SQUASH GRILLED CHEESE

Make delicious vegetarian sandwiches by spreading mayonnaise on both sides of two slices of bread, top with your favorite melting cheese (such as Cheddar or Muenster), and add a large handful of leftover radicchio and squash salad. Close the sandwich and cook in a skillet until browned on both sides and the cheese is melted, about 1½ minutes per side (the mayonnaise will help the exterior brown). Serve with mustard and pickles. See the cover of the book if you need any convincing!

Winter

Brunch for a Crowd

SHEET PAN FRITTATA WITH ROASTED MUSHROOMS + RICOTTA

SPICED BANANA BROWN BREAD

SHREDDED CABBAGE SALAD WITH FETA + HERBS

CANTALOUPE WITH LIME + SALT

Grace and I moved into our old farmhouse in a December that kicked off a very long, snowy winter during which we did little more than stay in our pajamas and scrape years' worth of paint from old walls (and wonder if we hadn't slightly lost our minds). By the following December, we were feeling much more settled and really grateful for the new community we were beginning to become part of. To mark the occasion, we invited over all of our neighbors on New Year's Day for a combination brunch–open house party. We asked about thirty people, expecting many would be out of town or unable to make it, and they all said yes. My goal was to put together a menu that could be served completely at room temperature so all of the food could be made ahead of time. I also wanted to avoid any expensive ingredients since it was such a large crowd. I landed on this menu, and it's become one of my most treasured.

UP TO 1 MONTH AHEAD	Bake the Spiced Banana Brown Bread, wrap it in plastic wrap, place it in an airtight freezer bag, and freeze. Defrost at room temperature (it will take about a day) before serving.
UP TO 2 DAYS AHEAD	If you didn't bake far ahead, bake the Spiced Banana Brown Bread, wrap in plastic wrap, and store at room temperature. Peel, seed, and slice the melon, cover and store in the refrigerator. Shred the cabbage and store in an airtight bag in the refrigerator.
UP TO A FEW HOURS AHEAD	Make the frittata and the cabbage salad. Bring butter or cream cheese to room temperature for serving with the bread.
LAST MOMENT	Arrange the melon, slice the frittata and the bread, and serve.

Sheet Pan Frittata with Roasted Mushrooms + Ricotta

SERVES 8 TO 10

Do you know what the easiest dish is to make for a large group in the morning? This frittata. By using a sheet pan, you can roast the mushrooms in a nice even layer and then just pour some beaten eggs on top and that's that. Don't skip the parchment and be sure to oil the sides of the pan, too (these steps guarantee that those beautiful eggs will end up on your plate and not stuck to the pan). The frittata cooks uniformly because the sheet pan provides such a large and even surface. You could use other roasted vegetables here instead of mushrooms, or do a combination. Try sliced peppers and onions, maybe with a little cooked and crumbled Italian sausage, or stir roasted cherry tomatoes and tons of fresh basil into the eggs. Small cubes of butternut squash mixed with chopped fresh sage and bits of goat cheese scattered over the eggs would be good, too. Anything goes.

1½ lb [680 g] wild and/or cremini mushrooms, tough ends discarded, roughly chopped

¼ cup [60 ml] olive oil

Kosher salt

1 Tbsp minced fresh thyme leaves

16 eggs

Large handful of minced fresh Italian parsley leaves (a little bit of stem is fine!)

1 cup [240 g] fresh whole-milk ricotta cheese

Preheat your oven to 425°F [220°C]. Line a sheet pan with parchment paper.

Place the mushrooms on the prepared sheet pan. Drizzle with 3 Tbsp of the olive oil and sprinkle with a large pinch of salt and the thyme. Use your hands to toss everything together. This will look like a lot of mushrooms, but they shrink quite a bit when they roast. Roast the mushrooms, stirring occasionally, until tender, browned, and concentrated, about 30 minutes.

Meanwhile, put the eggs and parsley into a large bowl and season with 2 tsp salt. Whisk until well blended.

Use a pastry brush or a folded paper towel to wipe the sides of the pan with the remaining 1 Tbsp olive oil. Make sure the mushrooms are in a nice even layer and then pour the beaten eggs over them. Evenly dollop the ricotta on top of the eggs.

Return the sheet pan to the oven and bake until the eggs are just set and a little bit puffed, about 15 minutes. Let the frittata cool for at least 10 minutes before cutting into squares for serving. It's equally good at room temperature.

Spiced Banana Brown Bread

SERVES 8 TO 10

This loaf, a cross between whole wheat brown bread and good old banana bread, is my preferred way to use up overripe bananas. Unlike many banana breads, this loaf isn't too dense or oily. Made with all whole wheat flour and sweetened ever so slightly with maple syrup, this is also bona fide healthy. Serve with soft butter or cream cheese. You can also stir some honey, maple syrup, or molasses into your butter or cream cheese. If you like nuts in your bread, stir a large handful of chopped nuts into the batter just before it goes into the pan. Walnuts or pecans are especially good.

2 cups [280 g] whole wheat flour

2 tsp baking powder

1 tsp baking soda

1 tsp kosher salt

1 Tbsp ground cinnamon

1 Tbsp ground ginger

½ tsp ground cloves

2 superripe bananas, peeled

2 eggs, lightly beaten

1 cup [240 ml] buttermilk

½ cup [160 g] maple syrup

1 Tbsp vanilla extract

Preheat your oven to 350°F [180°C]. Spray a 9-by-5-in [23-by-12-cm] loaf pan with baking spray. Line the bottom with parchment paper. Spray the parchment paper for good measure and set the pan aside.

In a large bowl, whisk together the flour, baking powder, baking soda, salt, cinnamon, ginger, and cloves.

Put the bananas into a large bowl and mash with a fork until broken up really well. Add the eggs, buttermilk, maple syrup, and vanilla and whisk until thoroughly mixed. Fold the flour mixture into the banana mixture just until combined. Use a rubber spatula to scrape the batter into the prepared pan and then smooth the surface so it is even.

Bake the bread until dark brown on top, firm to the touch, incredibly fragrant, and a toothpick inserted in the center comes out clean, about 50 minutes. Let the bread cool in the pan on a wire rack to room temperature. Once cooled, lift the bread out of the pan and then peel off and discard the parchment. Slice and serve. Leftovers can be wrapped tightly in plastic wrap and stored at room temperature for up to 4 days (these slices are best when toasted before serving).

Shredded Cabbage Salad with Feta + Herbs

SERVES 8 TO 10

This salad has all of the qualities I like in a recipe: colorful, affordable (thank you, cabbage!), crunchy, full of flavor, and, because it sits well, very friendly for entertaining. You can make it up to a few hours ahead of time and it will not suffer, which means you won't either. This is equally great served with the Grilled Beef + Zucchini Meatballs with Tahini Dressing (page 257) or even alongside a store-bought rotisserie chicken. Any leftovers are wonderful tucked inside a warm pita that you've slathered with hummus.

¼ cup plus 2 Tbsp [90 ml] olive oil

2 Tbsp cumin seeds

2 Tbsp fennel seeds

2 garlic cloves, minced

1½ lb [680 g] green cabbage, cored and thinly sliced (about ½ small head)

1 lb [455 g] red cabbage, cored and thinly sliced (about ½ small head)

¼ cup [60 ml] red wine vinegar, plus more as needed

Kosher salt

¼ cup [60 ml] fresh lemon juice, plus more as needed

4 large handfuls roughly chopped fresh soft herbs (cilantro, parsley, mint, dill, and/or chives all work well)

6 oz [170 g] feta cheese, crumbled

In a small skillet or saucepan over medium heat, combine the olive oil, cumin and fennel seeds, and garlic. Cook, stirring, until the spices sizzle and the garlic just begins to soften, about 2 minutes. Set the mixture aside to cool down slightly.

Meanwhile, put both cabbages into a large bowl, drizzle with the vinegar, and sprinkle with 1 tsp salt. Use your hands to scrunch everything together, working the vinegar and salt into the cabbage so the cabbage softens slightly.

Pour the warm oil mixture and the lemon juice over the cabbage. Sprinkle with another 1 tsp salt and add the herbs. Give everything a good stir, taste, and season with more salt, vinegar, and/or lemon juice if needed. Transfer half of the cabbage to a large, wide serving bowl and sprinkle with half of the feta cheese. Top with the remaining cabbage and then the remaining feta. Serve the salad within 4 hours. Cover and refrigerate any leftovers for up to 3 days.

Cantaloupe with Lime + Salt

This is not a recipe, obviously, but just a suggestion on how to serve a big platter of cantaloupe at a brunch party with lime wedges for squeezing over. It couldn't be simpler, but the combination of sweet melon and tart lime is exceptional, as is the striking color contrast. Plus, you can have a friend slice the melon while you busy yourself with other things. For a group of eight to ten folks, I would suggest 2 medium cantaloupes (choose the heaviest and most fragrant melons you can find). Peel and seed them and cut into bite-size pieces, which will be easy for your guests to eat. Squeeze a juicy lime over the melon pieces so they are kissed with tart juice and then scatter lime wedges around the plate because they look beautiful and they encourage more lime squeezing. A sprinkle of flaky sea salt and you're good to go (it makes the melon taste extra sweet).

It's Me Again

RICOTTA FRITTATA SANDWICHES

Leftover Sheet Pan Frittata with Roasted Mushrooms + Ricotta can be turned into delicious sandwiches. Focaccia, split in half horizontally so it opens like a book, is the easiest bread to use. Spread a bit of fresh ricotta on the bottom, pile the frittata on top, and finish with a little arugula lightly dressed with olive oil and lemon juice (or try the Kale Salad with Pepita Dressing on page 46). Cover with the top piece of focaccia and slice into individual portions. Great fare for a picnic or school! Of course, you can do individual rolls instead, or you can try open-faced sandwiches on thick slices of toasted country bread that you rub with a garlic clove before slathering with ricotta.

BANANA BREAD FRENCH TOAST

Leftover Spiced Banana Brown Bread can be repurposed into decadent French toast. It's actually worth baking an extra loaf just to be sure you can make this. For every serving of French toast, beat an egg with a splash of half-and-half and a healthy shake of ground cinnamon. Dip slices of the banana bread in the egg mixture and panfry in butter. Serve with sliced bananas, whipped cream, and a drizzle of maple syrup. Yum.

COUSCOUS + CABBAGE SALAD

Mix leftover Shredded Cabbage Salad with Feta + Herbs with an equal amount of cooked and cooled couscous to make a bright and colorful salad. Any cooked grain—barley, brown rice, quinoa—works well here.

LITTLE CABBAGE HAND PIES

Buy or prepare a basic piecrust (my go-to recipe is in *Small Victories*, the crust that tops the Chicken + Pea Skillet Pie). Roll it out so that it's pretty thin and use a juice glass to cut it into rounds. Cover about half of each round with a little handful of leftover cabbage salad (feta and all). Fold the other half over on each round to form half-moons. Use a fork to crimp and seal the edges. Transfer to a parchment-lined sheet pan. Lightly beat an egg with 2 Tbsp of water and brush each pie with it. Bake in a 400°F [200°C] oven until golden brown, about 20 minutes. Serve warm or at room temperature.

EASIEST CANTALOUPE SORBET

Place any leftover cantaloupe on a parchment-lined plate (or other flat surface) and freeze. Once the pieces are frozen, place them in a food processor and purée until smooth (if they're super solid, let them soften for 5 to 10 minutes first). Sweeten to taste with honey and serve immediately.

Chili + Cornbread Lunch

CHICKEN + BLACK-EYED PEA CHILI

SKILLET CORNBREAD WITH CHEDDAR + SCALLIONS

ROMAINE + CELERY SALAD WITH BUTTERMILK RANCH DRESSING

CARAMELIZED BANANAS WITH SOUR CREAM + BROWN SUGAR

My parents live a little over an hour away, which means they're the perfect lunch distance. They can drive up in the middle of the day for a meal and get back to their house in time to walk their dog (our family revolves around our pets quite a bit). I love serving this meal for them because they love it, and it's relaxed and comforting both to cook and to eat. I always make the chili the day before (it tastes even better that way), and it's fun to put little bowls of avocado, shredded cheese, sour cream, and scallions out on the table so we can top our own serving however we want. A little interaction like that is always nice.

The chili is also a great excuse to make the cornbread (!), and the salad is crunchy and bright and cuts through everything perfectly. The dessert is a nod to how much my mother likes the combination of bananas and sour cream, and it means you can go ahead and buy a big container of sour cream for the meal and know it will be put to good use.

UP TO 1 MONTH AHEAD	Make the chili and freeze it. Defrost overnight in the refrigerator and warm on the stove before serving.
UP TO 3 DAYS AHEAD	If you didn't go the freezer route, make the chili and store covered in the refrigerator (it's always better to make it ahead!). Make the salad dressing.
UP TO 1 DAY AHEAD	Wash the lettuce and slice the celery, wrap in ever-so-damp paper towels in sealed plastic bags, and store in the refrigerator.
UP TO A FEW HOURS AHEAD	Bake the cornbread.
LAST MOMENT	Heat the chili, stick the cornbread in a 300°F [150°C] oven to warm up, and set out the toppings for the chili. Dress the salad.
	Make the bananas.

Chicken + Black-Eyed Pea Chili

SERVES 4

This chicken chili is a testament to a well-stocked pantry (cheers to short grocery lists!). It turns staples like onions, spices, and canned tomatoes and beans into a family-friendly meal. The secret ingredient is the splash of brine from a jar of pickled jalapeños (which could also be distilled white vinegar) that gets stirred in right before serving. It doesn't make the chili spicy. Instead, it just kind of perks everything up and adds that extra dimension that happens when something acidic touches something slowly cooked (think about pineapple on *carnitas* or apple cider vinegar on pulled pork—speaking of which, check out page 153).

2 Tbsp olive oil

1½ lb [680 g] boneless, skinless chicken breasts and/or thighs, cut into bite-size pieces

2 tsp kosher salt

1 large red onion, finely diced

2 bell peppers (whatever color you like), stemmed, seeded, and finely diced

4 garlic cloves, minced

1 Tbsp ground cumin

1 Tbsp red chile powder

1 Tbsp dried oregano

One 28-oz [794-g] can whole peeled tomatoes

One 15½-oz [445-g] can black-eyed peas

3 Tbsp pickling liquid from jar of pickled jalapeño chiles, or 1½ Tbsp distilled white vinegar

Hot sauce, sour cream, grated Cheddar cheese, sliced avocado, cilantro, pickled jalapeño chiles, and sliced scallions for serving (all optional)

In a large, heavy pot heated over medium-high heat, warm the olive oil. Add the chicken in a single layer, working in batches if necessary, and sprinkle with 1 tsp of the salt (divide the salt between the batches if necessary). Cook, stirring now and then, until browned all over, about 15 minutes. Add the onion, bell peppers, garlic, cumin, chile powder, and oregano and cook, stirring now and then, until the vegetables begin to soften and brown in spots, about 10 minutes. Add the tomatoes with their juice, the black-eyed peas with their liquid, and the remaining 1 tsp salt. Bring the mixture to a boil and then immediately lower the heat to a gentle simmer.

Cover with the lid slightly ajar to let some steam escape. Cook, stirring now and then and breaking up the tomatoes as you stir, until all of the flavors have melded and the chicken is very tender, about 1 hour. (If you're using thighs, the meat will begin to shred.) Add the pickled jalapeño liquid, then taste the chili and add more jalapeño liquid and/or salt if needed. (If you can, let the chili cool down, then cover and refrigerate it overnight and reheat it the next day. The flavor will be even better.)

If using, set out the hot sauce, sour cream, Cheddar cheese, avocado, cilantro, pickled jalapeños, and scallions. Serve the chili piping hot.

Skillet Cornbread
with Cheddar + Scallions

SERVES 6 TO 8

Years of cornbread trial and error have brought me to one recipe that is rich but not just cake going by another name (which so much cornbread is). It's slightly tangy thanks to buttermilk and sharp Cheddar cheese, but it's just as good without the cheese if you prefer it less adorned. The best and most important part is the piping-hot cast-iron skillet. It's impossible to get the beautiful crust on the cornbread without it. Be sure to park the skillet in the oven when you turn it on so it can heat up while you're measuring and mixing.

1 cup [120 g] all-purpose flour

1 cup [140 g] stone-ground yellow cornmeal

3 Tbsp sugar

2 tsp baking powder

2 tsp kosher salt

2 eggs

1¼ cups [300 ml] buttermilk

7 Tbsp [100 g] unsalted butter, melted and cooled

¾ cup [75 g] coarsely grated sharp white Cheddar cheese

6 scallions, roots and dark green tops trimmed off, white and light green parts thinly sliced

Preheat your oven to 425°F [220°C]. At the same time, place an 8-in [20-cm] cast-iron skillet in the oven to get it really hot.

In a large bowl, whisk together the flour, cornmeal, sugar, baking powder, and salt. In a medium bowl, whisk together the eggs, buttermilk, and 6 Tbsp [85 g] of the butter until well blended. Pour the egg mixture into the flour mixture and stir everything well to combine. Stir in the cheese and scallions.

Carefully take the skillet out of the oven and add the remaining 1 Tbsp butter to it. Tilt the skillet to spread the butter evenly over the bottom and sides. Use a rubber spatula to scrape the batter into the skillet and smooth it into an even layer. Return the skillet to the oven and turn down the oven temperature to 400°F [200°C]. Bake the cornbread until it's beautifully golden brown, firm to the touch, and a toothpick inserted in the center comes out clean, about 30 minutes.

Let the cornbread cool for at least 10 minutes. Serve warm or at room temperature, cut into wedges. It is best served straight from the skillet. Store any leftovers in an airtight container at room temperature for up to 3 days (toast before serving).

Romaine + Celery Salad with Buttermilk Ranch Dressing

SERVES 4

I love this salad because it's so crunchy and it's always nice to eat something that feels fresh and light during winter, especially alongside something rich like chili. The dressing uses some of the buttermilk you'll likely have in the refrigerator if you make the cornbread. While I try never to call for two similar ingredients when you can get by with just one, I've tried this with just fresh garlic and just garlic powder. On their own, each is good, but the combination is what makes this taste like true ranch dressing (without all of the weird additives).

¼ cup [60 ml] buttermilk

2 Tbsp mayonnaise

2 tsp red wine vinegar

1 small garlic clove, minced

½ tsp garlic powder

½ tsp kosher salt

Small handful of minced fresh chives

3 hearts romaine lettuce, leaves separated

3 large celery stalks, thinly sliced on the diagonal

½ tsp coarsely ground black pepper

In a large bowl, whisk together the buttermilk, mayonnaise, vinegar, minced garlic, garlic powder, salt, and chives. Place the romaine and celery on top. At this point you can cover the bowl with a kitchen towel and let it sit for a couple of hours in the refrigerator. Right before serving, gently toss everything together. Sprinkle with the pepper and serve immediately.

Caramelized Bananas with Sour Cream + Brown Sugar

SERVES 4

My mother's affection for sour cream is enormous and stems from her most beloved childhood dessert: a bowl of sliced bananas topped with sour cream and brown sugar. Although there's nothing wrong with that no-fuss combination that requires zero cooking, this preparation brings in a hot skillet to create some irresistible caramel on the bananas. This one's for you, Mom.

¾ cup [180 g] sour cream

4 Tbsp [50 g] packed dark brown sugar

Kosher salt

½ tsp vanilla extract

2 Tbsp unsalted butter

4 bananas, peeled and halved lengthwise

In a medium bowl, whisk together the sour cream, 2 Tbsp of the brown sugar, a pinch of the salt, and the vanilla, mixing well. Set aside.

In a large nonstick skillet, melt the butter over medium-high heat. Place the bananas, cut-side down, in the hot pan and sprinkle with the remaining 2 Tbsp brown sugar and a pinch of salt. Cook the bananas without bothering them until the undersides are nicely caramelized, about 2 minutes.

Carefully transfer the bananas, cut-side up, to a serving platter. Dollop the sour cream mixture on top of the bananas and drizzle with the caramelized sugar left in the pan. Serve immediately while the bananas are warm and the sour cream is cold and your guests are ready for something sweet.

It's Me Again

CHILI NACHOS

Position an oven rack about 6 in [15 cm] from the heat source and preheat your broiler. Place an even layer of tortilla chips on a sheet pan. Top each chip with a spoonful of warmed leftover chili and then cover the whole thing with grated Cheddar cheese. Broil just until the cheese is melted. You could also use the cheese sauce from Simplest + Best Nachos on page 180. Remove the nachos from the broiler and sprinkle with a little minced raw onion and finely chopped fresh cilantro. Serve immediately with lots of napkins and cold margaritas (check out the pineapple ones on page 234).

CORNBREAD STUFFING

Leftover Skillet Cornbread with Cheddar + Scallions can be turned into stuffing that is so good that it's an excuse to make a second cornbread. Crumble whatever cornbread is left into bite-size pieces (it's okay if there are a lot of crumbs). For four servings, finely dice 1 yellow onion and 2 celery stalks and sauté in 2 Tbsp unsalted butter until softened. In a bowl, combine the sautéed vegetables with 4 large handfuls of crumbled cornbread, a large handful of chopped fresh Italian parsley, and about 6 minced large fresh sage leaves and mix well. Transfer the mixture to a baking dish in an even layer. Whisk together 1 egg and ¾ cup [180 ml] chicken or vegetable stock and drizzle over the cornbread mixture. Bake uncovered in a 375°F [190°C] oven until the top is golden brown, about 20 minutes. Serve with roast chicken.

SPICY STIR-FRIED LETTUCE + CELERY WITH GARLIC

Leftover romaine and celery from the salad can be turned into a side dish or a vegetarian main dish. For each serving, mince a garlic clove and about 1 tsp peeled fresh ginger. Heat a slick of neutral oil in a very hot skillet and add the garlic, ginger, and a large pinch of red pepper flakes. As soon as they start to sizzle, add a thinly sliced celery stalk and season with salt. When the celery begins to soften, add a few thinly sliced romaine leaves and cook just until they wilt, about 1 minute. Season with soy sauce and serve immediately. Excellent on rice with a fried egg.

Steak House Dinner for Vegetarians

MAPLE SYRUP OLD-FASHIONEDS

STUFFED MUSHROOMS WITH WALNUTS, GARLIC + PARSLEY

ICEBERG WEDGE SALAD WITH PICKLED SHALLOTS

CHARRED BROCCOLI WITH CAPERS + LEMON

DOUBLE-BAKED POTATOES WITH HORSERADISH + CHEDDAR

BLACK FOREST CAKE

I've always had a theory that steak houses are great places to take vegetarians (this from a girl whose regular diner order in college was a veggie burger with bacon on top, so my views on vegetarianism are, needless to say, flexible). They have the best and most satisfying salads and side dishes, making them surprisingly welcome places for folks who don't eat meat. I especially like the idea of any meatless meal that isn't obviously *vegetarian*. Do you know what I mean? So many vegetarian meals push the kale and quinoa, and, while I love those things, I think there's something really appealing about a rich, slightly over-the-top meal that just happens not to involve any meat. This is an appealing menu to make because so much of it can be done in advance, giving you time to fix yourself a cocktail while you wait for your friends to arrive.

UP TO 3 DAYS AHEAD	Assemble the stuffed mushrooms up to the point of baking them, cover, and refrigerate.
UP TO 1 DAY AHEAD	Make the salad dressing (minus the pickling liquid, add it day of) and the pickled shallots for the salad. Cut the iceberg into wedges and store wrapped in ever-so-damp paper towels in a sealed plastic bag in the refrigerator.
	Cut the broccoli into florets and mix the caper mixture. Cover and store separately in the refrigerator.
	Assemble the double-baked potatoes up to the point of the second bake.
	Bake the cake (don't top it yet), wrap it in plastic wrap, and store at room temperature.
UP TO A FEW HOURS AHEAD	Whip the cream for the cake and keep it in a bowl in the refrigerator (you might give it an extra whisking right before serving). Whisk together the cherry preserves mixture and keep it covered at room temperature.
LAST MOMENT	Pop the mushrooms in the oven while you mix the cocktails (or have a friend mix the drinks!). Serve them together while you roast the broccoli and give the potatoes their second bake in the oven. Add the pickling liquid and dress the salad.
	Top the cake with the whipped cream and cherry preserves mixture, then slice and serve it.

Maple Syrup Old-Fashioneds

MAKES 4

An old-fashioned typically starts with a sugar cube, but I like using maple syrup. It dissolves more easily and offers more flavor than just *sweet*. Fun story: When I was doing the photos for this book, my parents stopped by to say hi. My mother, who rarely if ever drinks, took a sip of one of these and loved it so much that she finished the whole thing. Rochelle-approved!

4 half-moon orange slices

2½ Tbsp maple syrup

12 dashes of Angostura bitters

½ cup [120 ml] club soda

¾ cup [180 ml] whiskey (or bourbon or rye, depending on your preference)

Ice, for serving

4 high-quality cocktail cherries (Luxardo cherries are the best, if a bit expensive)

Put the orange slices, maple syrup, and Angostura bitters in the bottom of a pitcher. Use the handle end of a wooden spoon (or a muddler if you have one) to mash everything together well. Stir in the club soda and whiskey. Fill four highball glasses with ice and divide the mixture between them (make sure each one gets a slice of orange). Top each drink with a cherry and serve immediately.

Stuffed Mushrooms
with Walnuts, Garlic + Parsley

SERVES 4 AS A NOSH WITH DRINKS

I started making these stuffed mushrooms as a Thanksgiving appetizer a few years ago when we had a few vegetarians at our table. I wanted to be able to offer them something rich and warm when they walked in. It turns out that everyone, not just vegetarians, love these. And they're so simple. If you want to be really organized, you can stuff the mushrooms a few days ahead of time, refrigerate them, and then pop them in the oven when the doorbell rings. The walnut mixture also makes a great topping for pasta or roasted vegetables. If you leave out the cheese, these mushrooms become vegan and are still quite delicious.

¼ cup [30 g] walnut halves

A large handful of fresh Italian parsley leaves (a little bit of stem is fine!)

1 large garlic clove, minced

3 Tbsp coarsely grated Parmesan or pecorino cheese

½ tsp kosher salt

2 Tbsp olive oil

12 small cremini or button mushrooms, stemmed

Preheat your oven to 400°F [200°C]. Line a small sheet pan or baking dish with parchment paper and set it aside.

Put the walnuts, parsley, garlic, cheese, and salt into a food processor, in that order. Pulse until everything is finely chopped. Add the olive oil and pulse to combine.

Use a small spoon to distribute the walnut mixture evenly among the mushrooms, placing it in the cavities the now-gone stems left behind. Line up the mushrooms, stuffed-sides up, on the prepared sheet pan.

Roast the mushrooms until softened and the tops are lightly browned, about 15 minutes. Let the mushrooms cool for a few minutes, then serve warm.

Iceberg Wedge Salad with Pickled Shallots

SERVES 4

I am an unabashed member of team iceberg. There's nothing like it when it comes to refreshing crunch. Like many other card-carrying members of the club, I especially enjoy cutting it into big wedges and blanketing it with blue cheese dressing. The pickled shallots on top of the salad might sound complicated, but they are actually easy to make, and, because they are tart and bright, they help offset the richness of the blue cheese. Plus, the pickling liquid becomes the base for the dressing, and I always love a two-for-one.

2 Tbsp red wine vinegar

2 Tbsp water

¼ tsp sugar

¼ tsp kosher salt, plus more as needed

1 large or 2 small shallots, thinly sliced

½ cup [120 g] mayonnaise

½ tsp freshly ground black pepper

½ cup [60 g] crumbled blue cheese

1 large head iceberg lettuce, quartered into wedges

3 large radishes, trimmed and thinly sliced

In a small, shallow bowl, whisk together the vinegar, water, sugar, and salt until the sugar and salt dissolve. Add the shallots, stir to combine, and let sit for at least 15 minutes to soften a bit, giving them a stir once or twice (or cover and refrigerate for up to 24 hours).

Drain the shallots, capturing the pickling liquid in a medium bowl. Add the mayonnaise and pepper to the pickling liquid and whisk well to combine. Stir in the cheese, then taste and season with salt if needed.

Place an iceberg wedge on each of four serving dishes (or put them all on one large serving platter). Evenly drizzle the dressing on the wedges, making sure you get plenty of blue cheese on each one. Divide the pickled shallots and radishes evenly among the wedges. Serve immediately.

Charred Broccoli with Capers + Lemon

SERVES 4

This is one of my most reliable side dishes and goes well with just about everything. You can also toss it with cooked pasta, sprinkle some cheese on top, and call it dinner. Speaking of cheese, it's excellent with some scattered on top (especially Parmesan or pecorino), but I didn't call for any here because it's part of a menu that includes both a salad and baked potatoes that are heavy on cheese. To make this dish spicy, sprinkle a large pinch (or more) of red pepper flakes on the broccoli before roasting or add some minced fresh chile or pickled jalapeño to the caper mixture. One last note: this recipe works equally well with cauliflower.

1 lb [455 g] broccoli, tough stems discarded, cut into large florets

3 Tbsp olive oil

½ tsp kosher salt

1 garlic clove, minced

2 Tbsp drained brined capers

2 Tbsp fresh lemon juice

Preheat your oven to 425°F [220°C]. At the same time, place a sheet pan in the oven to heat.

Meanwhile, put the broccoli into a large bowl, drizzle with 2 Tbsp of the olive oil, and sprinkle with the salt. Toss everything well to combine.

Once the oven comes to temperature, place the broccoli on the hot sheet pan in an even layer. Reserve the bowl. Roast the broccoli, stirring it now and then, until softened, browned, and crisp on the edges, about 30 minutes.

While the broccoli roasts, put the remaining 1 Tbsp olive oil, the garlic, capers, and lemon juice into the reserved bowl and stir well to combine.

Transfer the charred broccoli to the bowl and toss to coat evenly with the caper mixture. Serve warm or at room temperature.

Double-Baked Potatoes with Horseradish + Cheddar

SERVES 4, GENEROUSLY

When I was growing up, my babysitter Jennie used to make double-baked potatoes regularly, which I adored. What I didn't realize then was that Jennie made them because they were so practical. She would prepare them early in the day and then just warm them later and that was that. If you'd like to do that with these, just give them an extra 10 minutes or so during their second bake so they're hot through and through. I put tons of horseradish and sharp Cheddar cheese in them, plus lots of bright green scallions and parsley to make them look vaguely good for you. While they most definitely aren't, they're good for your spirit, and I think that counts for something. Like Jennie always says, "Child, life is short."

4 baking potatoes, each about ½ lb [230 g], scrubbed

2 Tbsp unsalted butter, cubed

1 tsp kosher salt

½ cup [120 g] sour cream

3 Tbsp prepared white horseradish

1 cup [100 g] coarsely grated sharp white Cheddar cheese

4 scallions, tough roots and dark green tops trimmed off, white and light green parts thinly sliced

A large handful of fresh Italian parsley leaves (a little bit of stem is fine!), finely chopped

Preheat your oven to 425°F [220°C].

Pierce each potato with a fork or a paring knife in a few places (this will help the steam escape as they cook). Place the potatoes directly on your oven rack and bake until easily pierced with a paring knife or a thin skewer, about 1¼ hours.

Transfer the potatoes to a cutting board but leave the oven on. Cut each potato in half lengthwise. Once they're cool enough to handle, scoop out nearly all of the potato flesh from each potato half, leaving enough in each half to create a sturdy shell (almost like a potato boat).

Transfer the scooped-out potato flesh to a large bowl and add the butter, salt, sour cream, horseradish, ½ cup [50 g] of the cheese, the scallions, and the parsley. Use a potato masher to crush everything together well, then give the mixture a few stirs with a large spoon to make sure all the ingredients are well mixed. Evenly divide the mixture among the potato shells (it's okay if they seem overstuffed; that makes them fun). Place the potatoes on a sheet pan and sprinkle the tops with the remaining ½ cup [50 g] cheese.

Return the potatoes to the oven. Roast until the tops are golden brown and crisp, about 15 minutes. Serve hot.

Black Forest Cake

SERVES 8 TO 10

Black Forest cake is traditionally made with layers of chocolate cake, frosting, and dark cherries (which must be pitted and cooked down). In other words, it's usually a feat. This version takes all of those flavors and simplifies them into a single, dense chocolate cake topped with whipped cream and store-bought cherry preserves—much easier! The cake, which is almost like a giant soufflé, is an old-fashioned flourless chocolate cake (which, by the way, makes this a gluten-free dessert and also a wonderful option for Passover). I first learned to make it from Jody Williams of Buvette (more about her on page 36). I have adjusted it a bit here so it uses slightly less butter and sugar, since fat and sweet come with the cream and cherry preserves.

The cake emerges from the oven puffy and inflated, but it quickly collapses when it cools down (this is not a bad thing, especially because it creates the perfect crater for toppings). I mix kirsch, a clear brandy flavored with sour cherries (very traditional in Black Forest cake), with the preserves to loosen them and add an extra kick. Light rum is a nice substitute, or if you prefer not to raid the liquor cabinet, add a spoonful each of water and lemon juice to the preserves. If you plan to bake the cake ahead, keep the whipped cream and preserves in the fridge and don't top the cake until just before you serve it.

½ cup plus 2 Tbsp [140 g] unsalted butter, cubed

1¾ cups [315 g] bittersweet chocolate chips (at least 60 percent cacao; see Note)

6 eggs, separated

½ tsp fresh lemon juice, distilled white vinegar, or apple cider vinegar

½ cup [100 g] sugar

½ tsp kosher salt

¾ cup [180 ml] heavy cream

2 tsp vanilla extract

½ cup [150 g] cherry preserves or jam

2 Tbsp kirsch (sour cherry brandy)

Preheat your oven to 350°F [180°C]. Spray the bottom and sides of a 9-in [23-cm] round cake pan with baking spray and line the bottom with a circle of parchment paper. Spray the parchment paper for good measure and set the pan aside.

Bring a small saucepan of water to a boil and then lower the heat to a simmer. Put the butter and chocolate into a large heatproof bowl and set it over the saucepan (make sure the bowl doesn't touch the water; if it does, pour some out). Stir the butter and chocolate until they are melted and smooth, about 3 minutes. Remove the bowl from the saucepan and let the mixture rest and cool while you tend to your eggs.

Put the egg whites into a stand mixer fitted with the whisk attachment (or use a handheld electric mixer or a whisk and some elbow grease) and beat on medium-high speed until they're foamy, about 30 seconds. With the

(Continued)

mixer still on medium-high speed, slowly pour in the lemon juice and ¼ cup [50 g] of the sugar and continue beating until the egg whites billow and turn into a white, fluffy, almost glossy cloud of stiff peaks, about another 2 minutes. To test if the egg whites are stiff enough, lift the whisk attachment. The whites that cling to it should stand nice and tall and not droop over (that's a soft peak). If they're not quite there yet, just keep mixing until they are. Transfer the egg whites to a separate bowl and hang on to them (if using a handheld electric mixer or whisk, just set the bowl with the egg whites aside).

Put the egg yolks, the remaining ¼ cup [50 g] sugar, and the salt into the same bowl you used for beating the whites (no need to wash it). (If using a handheld electric mixer or whisk, use a clean bowl.) Beat on medium-high speed until thick and pale yellow, about 1 minute. With the mixer still running on medium-high speed, slowly pour the chocolate mixture into the egg yolk mixture and mix well.

Use a rubber spatula to fold one-third of the beaten egg whites into the cake batter. It's okay if you sort of stir this one-third in rather than fold it in, as the cake batter is quite stiff and these egg whites will help lighten it. Add half of the remaining egg whites and gently and carefully fold them into the batter by cutting your spatula downward through the middle of the bowl, scraping it along the bottom of the bowl, and then pulling the mixture back up. Think of it like cutting in the egg whites and folding them with the batter. This helps preserve the air you worked hard to create in the egg whites. Fold in the rest of the egg whites the same way. Use the rubber spatula to scrape the batter into the prepared pan and then smooth the surface so it is even.

Bake the cake until it is puffed up, just barely firm to the touch, and a toothpick inserted in the center comes out with just a few dry crumbs clinging to it, about 40 minutes. The top might have some cracks. These will be covered soon with whipped cream, so not to worry. Set the cake aside on a wire rack to cool.

Combine the cream and vanilla in the stand mixer and beat on medium-high speed until soft peaks form, about 2 minutes (or use a bowl and a whisk and some solid effort). In a small bowl, whisk together the preserves and kirsch.

Use a dinner knife to loosen the edges of the cake from the pan sides and then invert it onto your work surface. Peel off and discard the parchment and then invert the cake one more time onto a serving platter. Spoon the whipped cream on top of the cake and then spoon the preserves mixture onto the cream.

Cut into wedges and serve. Leftovers can be covered and stored in the refrigerator for up to 3 days—good luck with that.

Note: If you can find only 10-oz [280-g] bags of bittersweet chocolate chips, you can buy just one bag and the recipe will still work just fine.

It's Me Again

PENNE AI FUNGI

Leftover stuffed mushrooms can be completely transformed into a wonderful pasta dish. You'll need 4 leftover stuffed mushrooms per portion. Scoop out the walnut filling and set it aside, then roughly chop the roasted mushrooms. Cook a diced small shallot or a handful of chopped leek in a skillet with a little knob of butter until softened and then add the chopped mushrooms and a splash of cream. Add a serving of al dente penne (or any other short, ridged shape that can catch all of the sauce) and toss to combine. If the pasta seems a little heavy, add a splash of the pasta cooking water. Serve sprinkled with the walnut filling and a bit of finely grated Parmesan or pecorino cheese. Done and done!

BROCCOLI FRITTERS

For every large handful of leftover broccoli, whisk together 1 egg, ½ cup [60 g] all-purpose flour, 2 Tbsp water, ½ tsp baking powder, and a pinch of salt. Finely chop the broccoli and stir into the batter. Cook the fritters in a buttered or oiled skillet as if making silver dollar pancakes. Excellent served with sour cream or plain Greek yogurt, especially if whisked with a squeeze of lemon juice and a few dashes of hot sauce.

SUPERRICH POTATO SOUP

Leftover double-baked potatoes can be turned into the richest soup ever. Start by finely chopping a large yellow onion and softening it with a little butter in a large pot. Add a few cups of vegetable or chicken stock. Peel off and discard the skins from whatever potatoes remain and then finely chop the potatoes and their stuffing and add to the stock. Bring to a simmer, stirring to break up the potatoes, and cook until the soup is warm and thick. If the soup is too thick, add a bit more stock. If you want it creamier (when you go all out, go!), add a splash of heavy cream. Serve hot. This is especially good if you've just been outdoors for a long time in cold weather.

CRISPY, CHEESY POTATO CAKES

Place leftover double-baked potatoes in a bowl and use a potato masher or your hands (messy, but fun) to crush them. Use your hands to form the mixture into little patties. Dust the patties with flour and cook in a lightly buttered nonstick skillet over medium-high heat until browned on both sides, about 1½ minutes per side. Serve hot.

Feast of the Almost Seven Fishes

CRAB TOASTS WITH LEMON + RED CHILE

BAGNA CAUDA WITH ENDIVE + FENNEL

SPAGHETTI WITH SCALLOPS, SQUID + SHRIMP

BOOZY LEMON SLUSHIES

I first heard about the feast of the seven fishes, the traditional Italian American Christmas Eve celebratory meal, from a girl on my Catholic middle-school basketball team (even though I am Jewish, I got to play on the team, and if that isn't a recipe for togetherness, I'm not sure what is). As a kid for whom a bowl of linguine with clams was my idea of heaven on earth (nope, I've never kept kosher), the feast of the seven fishes sounded like the greatest thing in the world. When I used to work as a private chef, I loved getting booked on Christmas Eve since it meant I could spend other people's money at the fish market. These days, I like making this pared-down menu that features five types of seafood because I think it's plenty. If you wanted it to be a true seven, add a pot of clams and mussels steamed open in a little white wine and garlic.

UP TO 1 DAY AHEAD	Cut the vegetables for the *bagna cauda*, wrap in ever-so-damp paper towels, and store in a plastic bag or an airtight container in the refrigerator.
UP TO A FEW HOURS AHEAD	Make the bagna cauda and keep covered at room temperature. Make the crab salad for the toasts, cover, and store in the refrigerator. Slice the bread for the toasts.
LAST MOMENT	Warm the bagna cauda and set it out with the vegetables. Assemble the crab toasts. Prepare the spaghetti. Make the slushies.

Crab Toasts with Lemon + Red Chile

SERVES 4

This is a perfect appetizer: pieces of garlic-rubbed toast spread with mayonnaise and topped with a bright, lemony crab salad. Because the toasts are so simple, the quality of the crab is important. I know it's an expensive ingredient, but you don't need a ton here and it's intended to be a celebratory meal. If you can't find amazing crab, you can substitute roughly chopped cooked lobster or shrimp or even high-quality canned tuna or salmon. A quick apology and note: I didn't put the red chile in the crab salad in the photo, so if you're looking for bits of red, they're absent! Please add to yours for a lovely, lively kick (and feel free to omit if you're not into spice).

½ lb [230 g] jumbo lump crabmeat, picked over for shell fragments

Finely grated zest and juice of 1 large lemon

2 Tbsp olive oil

1 Tbsp minced fresh red chile or red chile paste (like sambal oelek)

A small handful of minced fresh Italian parsley leaves (a little bit of stem is fine!)

Kosher salt

4 large slices country bread (I like these thick, about 1 in/2.5 cm)

1 garlic clove

4 Tbsp [60 g] mayonnaise

In a large bowl, combine the crabmeat, lemon zest and juice, olive oil, chile, and parsley. Mix well and season to taste with salt. Reserve the mixture.

Toast the bread until dark brown (use your toaster oven, broiler, or even outdoor grill). Rub one side of each piece of toast with the garlic clove. The crunchy surface of the bread will act almost as a grater and catch little bits of the garlic. You're looking to impart just a whiff of garlic flavor to the bread, not mash the garlic into it, so use a light hand here. Discard whatever little bit of garlic is left over or use it for something else (pretty much anything else in this book because I put it in everything and have even been known to wrap ½ garlic clove in plastic wrap for use later).

Spread 1 Tbsp of the mayonnaise on the garlic-rubbed side of each piece of toast and then divide the crab salad evenly among the toasts. Drizzle any juice from the bottom of the crab bowl over the salad. Cut each toast into a few pieces so it's easier to eat. Serve immediately.

Bagna Cauda with Endive + Fennel

SERVES 4

Bagna cauda means "warm bath" and how could anyone resist that? It's a traditional Italian dip made of olive oil, garlic, and anchovies. Some folks swear by adding butter, while others think olive oil only is the way to go. I am a big fan of *and* instead of *or*, so I use some of both. You could also add some lemon peel or a pinch of red pepper flakes, but I like keeping things simple. Serve this warm bath with lots of crisp, cold vegetables. I use Belgian endive and fennel here, but use whatever you like and whatever you have (radicchio leaves are wonderful, as are radishes and blanched cauliflower florets). If you make this earlier in the day, let the mixture cool in the saucepan, then when it's time to serve, warm the dip over low heat.

½ cup [120 ml] olive oil

2 Tbsp unsalted butter

3 garlic cloves, minced

One 2-oz [55-g] can olive oil–packed anchovy fillets

2 large heads Belgian endive, leaves separated

1 large fennel bulb, cut lengthwise into thin wedges

In a small saucepan over medium-low heat, combine the olive oil, butter, garlic, and the entire contents of the anchovy can (oil and all). Cook, stirring to break up the anchovies, until the garlic softens and mellows and the mixture is almost cloudy and creamy, about 5 minutes.

Transfer to a shallow heatproof serving bowl and set the bowl on a large platter or board. Surround the bowl with the endive and fennel and serve immediately.

Spaghetti with Scallops, Squid + Shrimp

SERVES 4

If I see pasta with seafood on a menu, I have a hard time not ordering it. As it always feels festive, it's also a great dish to cook at home for a special occasion. Getting the timing right is important, however, so you don't end up with overcooked seafood or cold spaghetti. The best approach is to get everything ready (meaning, mince your garlic, cut up the squid, chop the parsley, and so on), cook the seafood while the pasta is boiling, and then combine them. Also, make sure that when the pasta drops, your guests are in their seats. This is not the kind of dish that waits for people to eat it. If you like, you can skip the spaghetti and just serve the seafood on its own, maybe with some grilled bread and garlicky broccoli rabe. You can also cook only one type of seafood (use 1½ lb/680 g total) or any combination you like. Put a little bowl of dried red pepper flakes on the table for anyone who wants a sprinkle.

Kosher salt

1 lb [455 g] spaghetti

¼ cup [60 ml] olive oil

½ lb [230 g] medium-large shrimp, peeled and deveined

8 sea scallops or 12 bay scallops, side muscles discarded

4 garlic cloves, minced

½ tsp red pepper flakes

½ lb [230 g] cleaned squid, bodies cut into narrow rounds and tentacles left whole

2 Tbsp unsalted butter

Finely grated zest and juice of 1 lemon

2 large handfuls of roughly chopped fresh Italian parsley leaves (a little bit of stem is fine!)

First thing, bring a large pot of water to a boil. Make sure everything else is ready to go once the water boils.

Season the water with plenty of salt (like a small handful; this is not the time for a pinch—think of it as seasoning the pasta). Drop the spaghetti into the water and set a timer for 2 minutes less than the lowest time the box tells you.

Meanwhile, set the largest skillet you have over high heat and add the olive oil. Once the oil is nice and hot, add the shrimp and scallops in as even a layer as possible. Season lightly with salt and cook until the undersides are golden brown, about 2 minutes. Flip the shrimp and scallops, sprinkle the garlic and red pepper flakes on top, and then add the squid to the pan. Cook, stirring now and then, until all of the seafood is firm to the touch and opaque, about 1½ minutes. Turn off the heat and stir in the butter.

(Continued)

Use a measuring cup (or a coffee mug) to reserve 1 cup [240 ml] of the pasta cooking water and then drain the spaghetti in a colander. Return the spaghetti to the now-empty pot, add the reserved cooking water, and then transfer the entire contents of the seafood skillet to the pot (it's easier to toss this large amount of stuff in a pot than in a skillet). Set the pot over low heat and cook, stirring with tongs, until the pasta absorbs quite a bit of the liquid, about 2 minutes. Stir in the lemon zest and juice and parsley.

Transfer to a large, wide serving bowl or to individual serving bowls and serve immediately. Make sure everyone gets their equal share of seafood.

Boozy Lemon Slushies

SERVES 4

This is the perfect no-dessert dessert and requires absolutely no effort. If you can open a bottle of wine, you can make these slushies. My only piece of advice is to take the lemon sorbet out of the freezer right before you remove the dinner plates from the table. That gives it time to soften while you clear the decks and have a chat with your friends.

4 scoops lemon sorbet

½ cup [120 ml] vodka, preferably chilled

2 cups [480 ml] sparkling wine (preferably Prosecco), preferably chilled

Get yourself four tall glasses and place a scoop of lemon sorbet in the bottom of each one. Add 2 Tbsp of the vodka to each glass and stir well to mix (let the mixture sit for a minute or two if the sorbet isn't soft enough to stir). Add ½ cup [120 ml] of the sparkling wine to each glass and stir again. Serve immediately with straws and spoons.

It's Me Again

BAGNA CAUDA CAESAR DRESSING

Take the leftover bagna cauda and whisk in a spoonful of mayonnaise, a splash of red wine vinegar, a squeeze of lemon juice, and a generous amount of finely grated Parmesan cheese. Taste as you mix, adding a little more of any of those ingredients until you get the consistency and flavor you like. Serve on romaine lettuce.

ROASTED FENNEL + ENDIVE

Place leftover fennel and endive in a baking dish and pour over whatever bagna cauda you have left over. Mix well to combine. Roast in a 400°F [200°C] oven until tender and browned in spots, about 25 minutes. Serve as is or topped with grated Parmesan cheese and/or toasted bread crumbs. It's an excellent side dish.

ROASTED RED CABBAGE WITH ANCHOVY + PINE NUTS

Thinly slice red cabbage as if you were making coleslaw. Toss with olive oil and salt and roast on a sheet pan in a 425°F [220°C] oven until softened and charred in spots, about 30 minutes. Serve drizzled with leftover bagna cauda and topped with toasted pine nuts.

CRAB CAKES

Leftover Crab Toasts with Lemon + Red Chile can be turned into delicious crab cakes. Finely chop the leftover toast (it's fine if it has mayonnaise on it) and mix with the leftover crab salad. Bind with extra mayonnaise and season to taste with salt and pepper. Form the mixture into small patties. Panfry the crab cakes in a medium-hot nonstick skillet slicked with a little olive oil. Serve on arugula dressed with lemon juice and olive oil.

KOREAN-STYLE COLD SEAFOOD SALAD

If you have leftover cooked seafood from the pasta (and/or extra crab you didn't use for the toasts), chill it in the refrigerator. Make a dressing out of equal parts gochujang (Korean red chile paste, or your favorite chile paste), soy sauce, sesame oil, and rice vinegar. Add a little minced garlic and season to taste with salt. Coat the seafood with the dressing. You could also mix in shredded napa cabbage. Sprinkle with toasted sesame seeds and serve.

BOOZY LEMON POUND CAKE

If you don't finish your slushies and/or if your lemon sorbet melts completely, soak slices of pound cake in the liquid. Serve with whipped cream.

A Not-Kosher Jewish Christmas

CRISPY SCALLION + SESAME PANCAKES

OVEN-STEAMED FISH WITH CRISPY GARLIC + RED CHILE OIL

STIR-FRIED ROASTED EGGPLANT WITH PORK

BABY BOK CHOY WITH SESAME SAUCE

TAKEOUT RICE

ORANGE WEDGES

Until I married Grace and started celebrating Christmas with her family, December 25 had always been the day I went to the movies with my family to see at least two (sometimes even three!) films back to back, followed by a trip to the local Chinese restaurant. Many lovingly refer to this itinerary as Jewish Christmas, since movie theaters and Chinese restaurants are pretty much the only businesses open on the holiday. This menu is an ode to the Christmases of my youth. It is also decidedly not-kosher as there is ground pork in the eggplant (which you can substitute with chicken or turkey or leave out). It also features one of my most unusual assignments for a guest: pick up cooked rice from your local Chinese restaurant on the way to the house for dinner. It's one less thing to cook and one less pot to clean, and it comes with the unquestionable guarantee that the rice will be perfectly cooked. Also, there's no recipe for the orange wedges because, well, just cut up some oranges.

UP TO 1 DAY AHEAD

Make and cook the pancakes, wrap them in aluminum foil, and keep at room temperature. Warm them in a 300°F [150°C] oven (still wrapped in the foil) before serving. Or make the dough up until the point you divide it into portions. Wrap the dough in plastic wrap and refrigerate for up to 24 hours, then let it come to room temperature before rolling out and cooking just before serving.

Cut the oranges into wedges, wrap in ever-so-damp paper towels, place in a plastic bag, and refrigerate.

Trim and wash the bok choy, wrap in ever-so-damp paper towels, place in a plastic bag, and refrigerate.

Roast the eggplant and reserve in a covered container in the refrigerator.

UP TO A FEW HOURS AHEAD

Set up your bok choy in its skillet.

Make the crispy garlic and red chile oil.

Pick up your takeout rice or make sure a friend is on it!

LAST MOMENT

Warm or cook the pancakes, and serve immediately. This is the kind of thing I like to serve at the kitchen counter before moving everyone over to the kitchen table. Enjoy them while you steam the fish in the oven, brown the pork and add the eggplant, and turn the heat on under the bok choy.

Crispy Scallion + Sesame Pancakes

SERVES 6

These crispy scallion pancakes have all of the traditional appeal of their restaurant namesakes, with more flavor and texture thanks to sesame oil and sesame seeds and less greasiness than what is often served in Americanized Chinese restaurants. They're also really fun to make because you must shape the dough a specific way to achieve lots of flaky layers, and it's basically like getting to fool around with Play-Doh. Once you have kneaded the dough, it must rest and relax for an hour before you roll it out. That's a good time for you to either do the same (doesn't that sound nice?) or get going on the rest of the menu.

1½ cups [180 g] all-purpose flour, plus more for dusting

1 Tbsp sesame seeds

1 tsp kosher salt

2 Tbsp toasted sesame oil

½ cup [120 ml] boiling water

¼ cup [60 ml] rice vinegar

3 Tbsp soy sauce

¼ cup [60 ml] canola or other neutral oil, plus more if needed

8 large scallions, tough roots and dark green tops trimmed off, white and light green parts thinly sliced

In a large bowl, stir together the flour, sesame seeds, salt, 1 Tbsp of the sesame oil, and the boiling water. The dough should just come together, but it will be far from smooth and instead quite shaggy and a bit dry. Although you might be tempted to add more water at this point, please resist, as the dough will come together beautifully once you knead it. If there are lots of crumbs and it's not coming together at all, you can add a tiny splash more water, 1 or 2 Tbsp at most (variables like how you measure your flour and the humidity in the room can affect the dough, and it's in these variables that the nuances of working with dough of all kinds live).

Lightly dust your work surface with flour. Transfer the dough to it and then shape the dough into a large ball. To knead the dough, press it with the heel of your hand, pushing it away from you. Immediately pull it back, folding the top of the dough back on itself. Kneading is all about this push-and-pull action. Give the dough a little clockwise turn each time you complete a push-and-pull sequence so it gets evenly worked, and knead it until its surface is completely smooth and the whole thing feels both solid and soft at the same time. It will take a full 5 minutes of kneading. If the dough sticks to your hands or the work surface as you're kneading, dust the surface with more flour.

Cover the dough with plastic wrap or a kitchen towel and let it relax for an hour. It won't rise much during that time, but it will be a lot more relaxed and easy to roll out because kneading develops gluten. Gluten is basically like an elastic band, and it is very hard to roll out an elastic band—or this dough—that's tightly wound (perhaps we could all use an hour to relax now and then?).

While the dough is resting, in a small bowl, whisk together the vinegar, soy sauce, and the remaining 1 Tbsp sesame oil. Reserve the mixture. This is also a good time to slice your scallions if you haven't already and set them aside.

Use a sharp knife to cut the dough into six equal pieces. Working with one piece of dough at a time, place it on your lightly floured surface and, using a rolling pin, roll it out into a thin circle about 8 in [20 cm] in diameter. Brush the surface with about 1 tsp of the canola oil and top with one-sixth of the scallions (about 3 Tbsp). Roll up the dough circle into a tight cylinder, as if rolling up a tiny yoga mat or making a cigar. Shape the cylinder into a tight coil (like coiling a rope) and tuck the little tail of the spiral underneath the dough. Use your trusty rolling pin to flatten the dough once again, this time into a slightly smaller circle about 6 in [15 cm] in diameter. If a few scallions pop out, don't worry. If the dough fights you at all and resists rolling, cover it with your plastic wrap or towel and let it rest for 10 minutes, then roll again. Repeat to make the remaining five pancakes.

Place a medium nonstick skillet over medium-high heat and add 1 Tbsp of the canola oil. When the oil is hot, add a pancake and cook, turning it a few times as it cooks, until golden brown and crispy on both sides, about 5 minutes total (don't be tempted to turn up the heat to high or the outside will cook before the inside gets a chance to cook). Repeat the process with the remaining pancakes, adding the remaining 1 Tbsp canola oil as needed, plus a little more if that runs out.

Cut the pancakes into wedges and serve immediately, with the soy sauce mixture on the side for dipping.

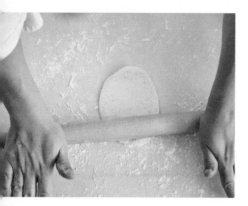

Oven-Steamed Fish
with Crispy Garlic + Red Chile Oil

SERVES 6

I often steam food not for any health reasons, but because it creates such clear flavors and the food cooks so gently. But when it comes to steaming fish, I find that a stove-top bamboo steamer (or other similar steamer) is a clunky way to cook more than one portion at a time. I devised this easy method of steaming fish on a sheet pan in the oven using just a little water. The crispy garlic provides wonderful texture, and in a full circle way, the garlicky oil you're left with becomes the base for the chile oil. I like to use a plain white fish, like sole or cod, for this dish, but you can use whatever you like, including salmon, mackerel, or grouper.

¼ cup [60 ml] canola or other neutral oil

6 large garlic cloves, very thinly sliced

Kosher salt

A large pinch of red pepper flakes

3 lb [1.3 kg] fish fillets (see headnote)

½ cup [120 ml] boiling water

2 Tbsp soy sauce

2 scallions, tough roots and dark green tops trimmed off, white and light green parts thinly sliced

Preheat your oven to 400°F [200°C].

Line a plate with paper towels and keep it close. In a small saucepan over medium-high heat, combine the oil and a slice of garlic. When the garlic slice starts to bubble around the edges, add the rest of the garlic slices. Fry, stirring continuously, until the garlic is light golden brown, about 2 minutes. Remove from the heat and use a slotted spoon to transfer the garlic to the paper towel–lined plate. Season the garlic with salt and set aside.

Add the red pepper flakes to the oil in the pan and return the pan to medium-high heat. Let the oil cook until the pepper flakes bubble, about 30 seconds. Turn off the heat and let the oil cool while you prepare the fish.

Brush a sheet pan with 1 Tbsp of the red chile oil and arrange the fish fillets in the pan in a single layer (it's okay if they overlap a little). Sprinkle each fillet with a little salt. Carefully pour the boiling water around the fish. Wrap the sheet pan tightly with aluminum foil.

Steam the fish in the oven until firm to the touch and the flesh is opaque and flakes easily when pierced with a paring knife (check by uncovering the pan), about 15 minutes for thin fillets like sole and up to 20 to 25 minutes for thicker fillets like salmon or grouper.

Use a fish spatula or slotted spoon to carefully transfer the fish to a warmed serving platter (discard the cooking liquid or save for another use such as chowder). Whisk the soy sauce into the remaining red chile oil (it's okay if it doesn't emulsify) and drizzle evenly over the fish. Top with the reserved crispy garlic and the scallions and serve immediately.

Stir-Fried Roasted Eggplant with Pork

SERVES 6

While eggplant is really a summer vegetable, it's easy to find in grocery stores year-round, and this deeply savory, wintry-feeling dish is one of my favorite ways to prepare it. I cut the eggplant into cubes and roast it, which is way less messy than frying and also much healthier (keep this in mind anytime you have a bunch of eggplant on hand). Then it gets stir-fried with gingery, caramelized pork and a splash of soy sauce. You can use ground turkey or chicken instead (please seek out the dark meat if so). Serve this dish on top of rice for a complete meal.

3½ lb [1.6 kg] eggplant (about 2 very large), ends trimmed, cut into 1-in [2.5-cm] cubes

6 Tbsp [90 ml] olive oil

2 tsp kosher salt

2 Tbsp canola or other neutral oil

1 lb [455 g] ground pork

¼ cup [35 g] peeled and minced or grated fresh ginger

½ tsp red pepper flakes

1 Tbsp soy sauce

¼ cup [60 ml] chicken stock or water

Position one rack in the center of your oven and a second rack in the top third and preheat to 425°F [220°C].

Divide the eggplant cubes between two sheet pans. Drizzle each pan with 3 Tbsp of the olive oil and sprinkle each pan with ½ tsp of the salt. Use your hands to mix everything together and then spread the eggplant in an even layer on each pan. I know it's tempting to put all of the eggplant on one sheet pan, but dividing it will keep it from steaming and ensure that all of it gets more color and texture. Roast the eggplant, stirring once or twice along the way and switching the pans between the racks and rotating them back to front halfway through roasting, until softened and browned, about 35 minutes. Set the eggplant aside.

Meanwhile, place the largest skillet you have (I'm talking at least 12 in/30.5 cm in diameter) over high heat and add the canola oil. When the oil is nice and hot, crumble the pork into the pan and sprinkle with the remaining 1 tsp salt. Cook the pork, stirring now and then, until it loses its rawness, releases lots of liquid, and is on its way to being browned, about 5 minutes. Add the ginger and red pepper flakes and cook, stirring, until the liquid has evaporated and the pork is browned and a little bit crisp, about 5 more minutes.

Add the roasted eggplant to the skillet and drizzle with the soy sauce and stock. Cook, stirring, just until everything is nicely combined and the liquid is mostly evaporated, about 2 minutes. Transfer to a serving dish and serve immediately.

Baby Bok Choy with Sesame Sauce

SERVES 6

Just like the fish steamed on a sheet pan in the oven, this method of steaming bok choy (which could easily be any vegetable) in a skillet is fast and easy. I especially love it because you can set up the skillet a few hours in advance, so all you need to do when you're ready to eat is turn on the heat. You can cook a combination of vegetables using this method, too; just put whatever takes longer to cook on the bottom (for example, carrots on the bottom and green beans on top, and a bit of butter on top is always welcome). The quick, rich sauce for the bok choy carries a double dose of flavor from the toasted sesame oil and the creamy tahini.

3 lb [1.3 kg] baby bok choy, tough outer leaves and root ends trimmed, halved lengthwise

½ cup [120 ml] water

½ tsp kosher salt

1 Tbsp toasted sesame oil

2 Tbsp tahini

2 tsp sesame seeds, toasted

Put the bok choy into the largest skillet you have (at least 12 in/30.5 cm in diameter). Add the water and sprinkle evenly with the salt. Cover the skillet and place over high heat. Once the water comes to a boil, cook just until the bok choy is bright green and barely tender, about 2 minutes.

Drain the bok choy, reserving ¼ cup [60 ml] of the cooking water, and transfer the bok choy to a serving bowl. Put the reserved cooking water into a small bowl and whisk in the sesame oil and tahini. Drizzle the bok choy with the mixture and sprinkle with the sesame seeds. Serve steaming hot.

It's Me Again

FISH + CRISPY GARLIC FRIED RICE

This is for your leftover cooked rice and Oven-Steamed Fish with Crispy Garlic + Red Chile Oil. Heat up a thin layer of neutral oil in a large nonstick skillet over medium-high heat. When it's nice and hot, crumble in whatever leftover cooked rice you have and season generously with salt and pepper. Cook, stirring it just a bit, until warmed through, about 2 minutes. Add whatever fish you have left, along with its crispy garlic and red chile oil, and then crack 1 or 2 eggs into the rice and cook, stirring, until the eggs are cooked. Season the fried rice to taste with soy sauce. Serve hot.

COLD RICE NOODLE + BOK CHOY SALAD

Cold leftover Baby Bok Choy with Sesame Sauce can be mixed with equal amounts of cooked and cooled rice noodles to make an easy salad. Dress with equal amounts rice vinegar, soy sauce, and fish sauce sweetened to taste with brown sugar or honey (or agave nectar—whatever you have). This is really nice topped with roughly chopped roasted peanuts or cashews.

EGGPLANT + PORK POTSTICKERS

Use leftover eggplant to fill store-bought dumpling wrappers. Make sure you seal the edges securely (wet with a little water first). Place a slick of canola oil (or any neutral oil) in a large nonstick pan set over medium-high heat. Add the potstickers to the skillet and cook until the undersides are browned, about 1½ minutes. Add a splash of water, cover, and cook until the wrappers are tender, about 2 minutes. Serve hot with soy sauce and rice vinegar for dipping.

LEFTOVER RICE

See pages 268 to 269 for so many ideas for things to do with your leftover cooked rice. From Brown Sugar Rice Pudding to Vietnamese Comfort Soup, I've got you covered.

Spring

NET WT
13 OZ (368g)

Easy All-Green Lunch

STRIPED BASS WITH BUTTER VERDE

CRUSHED POTATOES + PEAS

SAUTÉED ZUCCHINI WITH GREEN GODDESS DRESSING

PISTACHIO MANDELBROT COOKIES

When my mother was a bit younger than I am, she was the assistant art director at *New York* magazine and belonged to a group called the Underground Gourmet Society. The group had grown out of a column in the magazine created by Milton Glaser and Jerome Snyder called the "Underground Gourmet." The group began by going out to lunch to see and taste lots of dishes, and then later they started throwing dinner parties together. My mother and her colleagues would rotate apartments (not unlike my card night group on page 41) for meals that revolved around a theme, such as an all-white dinner to which people brought things like mashed potatoes and cauliflower. One legendary meal required every dish to be handheld. She was assigned the soup course. Always up for a creative challenge, my mother arrived at the party with "gazpachsicles."

I loved hearing stories about the Underground Gourmet Society when I was growing up and imagining the dinner parties I might throw one day. This menu, which could also be called Fifty Shades of Green, is an homage to the Underground Gourmet Society and to my mom who has taught me everything I know about a well-edited anything with a clear point of view. Note that I purposely call for only parsley and chives in these recipes, so one bunch of each will be used up for the meal. But you can use whatever fresh soft herbs you like in the fish, potatoes, and zucchini.

UP TO 3 DAYS AHEAD	Make the cookies and store in a tightly covered container at room temperature.
UP TO 1 DAY AHEAD	Wash all of the herbs and chop the zucchini, wrap them separately in ever-so-damp paper towels, put them in plastic bags or airtight containers, and store in the refrigerator. Make the green goddess dressing.
UP TO A FEW HOURS AHEAD	Cook the zucchini, drizzle with the dressing, and let sit, covered, at room temperature. It's just as delicious at room temperature as it is hot.
LAST MOMENT	Prepare the fish and potatoes.

Striped Bass with Butter Verde

SERVES 4

This is so simple and unbelievably delicious. The butter mixture is basically good old Italian *salsa verde* made with butter instead of olive oil (but hey, if you're opposed to butter, no worries; just use ¼ cup/60 ml olive oil). You can make this dish with one large piece of fish and then serve it broken into large pieces, or you can use individual-portion-size fillets (in which case the cooking time will be on the faster end of the range given in the recipe). I like striped bass here because it's firm and pretty sustainable, but use any type of fish that you like, preferably one that swims in water near you and is sold fresh. The butter mixture is also delicious drizzled on steamed clams.

2 Tbsp olive oil

1 lemon, ends trimmed, thinly sliced

2 lb [910 g] skin-on center-cut striped bass or other firm white fish fillet

¾ tsp kosher salt

4 Tbsp [55 g] unsalted butter

A small handful of fresh Italian parsley leaves (a little bit of stem is fine!), minced

2 Tbsp minced fresh chives

2 Tbsp drained brined capers

1 garlic clove, minced

Preheat your oven to 425°F [220°C].

Drizzle 1 Tbsp of the olive oil over the surface of a baking dish large enough to hold the fish and use your fingers to spread it to coat the bottom. Arrange the lemon slices in a single layer, overlapping them slightly, in the dish. These will be the bed for your fish. Place the fish, flesh-side up, on top of the lemon slices. Drizzle the remaining 1 Tbsp olive oil on top of the fish and sprinkle with ½ tsp of the salt.

Roast the fish until it is opaque and the blade of a paring knife feels hot after inserting it into the center of the fish, 10 to 25 minutes, depending on the thickness of the fish. (I know this is a broad range, but striped bass comes in a range of thicknesses; start checking at the 10-minute mark and go from there.)

While the fish is roasting, put the butter into a small skillet or pot set over medium heat. Once it melts, turn off the heat and stir in the parsley, chives, capers, garlic, and the remaining ¼ tsp salt.

Spoon the butter mixture over the cooked fish. I like to serve this straight from the baking dish in all of its rustic glory. Make sure to serve the lemon slices, too, as they are entirely edible and quite delicious in their own bitter, earthy way.

Crushed Potatoes + Peas

SERVES 4

When I was a kid, anytime mashed potatoes and peas were on my plate, I always combined the two. This happened most frequently—randomly enough!—at my summer camp, where "Thanksgiving dinner" was a very popular meal. From looking around at my friends' plates, I knew this potato-pea mash-up (quite literally) wasn't something particular to me. This side dish does the combining for you and is basically the easiest version of mashed potatoes ever because no peeling or chopping is involved. I *highly* recommend serving the fish (page 142) with all of its wonderful butter on top of these potatoes so they can absorb all of the extra butter.

1½ lb [680 g] small white creamer potatoes or fingerlings

3 tsp kosher salt, plus more as needed

One 10-oz [280-g] package frozen peas

2 Tbsp unsalted butter, cubed

¼ cup [60 ml] heavy cream

3 scallions, tough roots and dark green tops trimmed off, white and light green parts thinly sliced

A large handful of fresh Italian parsley leaves (a little bit of stem is fine!), finely chopped

In a large pot, combine the potatoes, 2 tsp of the salt, and water to cover by 1 in [2.5 cm]. Set the pot over high heat and bring the water to a boil. Lower the heat and simmer until the potatoes are tender (test with a paring knife), about 20 minutes. Add the peas to the pot and cook until bright green, about 30 seconds. Drain the potatoes and peas in a colander and shake them well to dry.

Return the potatoes and peas to the empty pot (no need to turn the stove on—just use the pot as a bowl because why dirty something else?). Add the butter, cream, half of the scallions, and half of the parsley. Sprinkle with the remaining 1 tsp salt and use a potato masher to crush everything together. The goal is to mix all of the ingredients well but not create smooth mashed potatoes. This dish is all about texture. Taste and adjust the seasoning with more salt if needed. Transfer the mixture to a serving bowl and sprinkle with the remaining scallions and parsley. Serve immediately.

Sautéed Zucchini with Green Goddess Dressing

SERVES 4

A lovely side dish, this zucchini also makes a delicious omelet or vegetarian taco filling. Top either with some avocado for extra green. For this meal, serve the zucchini warm or at room temperature. It's great either way and the latter means you can make it a few hours ahead of time.

¼ cup [60 g] plain full-fat Greek yogurt

A large handful of fresh Italian parsley leaves (a little bit of stem is fine!), roughly chopped

A large handful of minced fresh chives

1 garlic clove, minced

1 Tbsp white wine vinegar

¼ cup [60 ml] olive oil, plus 2 Tbsp, plus more as needed

Kosher salt

1½ lb [680 g] zucchini (about 3 large), ends trimmed

In a food processor, combine the yogurt, parsley, chives, garlic, vinegar, and ¼ cup [60 ml] of the olive oil and purée until smooth. You might need to scrape down the sides with a rubber spatula once or twice to make sure everything is evenly combined. Season the dressing to taste with salt and reserve it.

Cut each zucchini in half lengthwise. Then, working with one zucchini half at a time, lay it on its flat side so it's stable and cut into half-moons ½ in [12 mm] thick. You can do this on the diagonal if you'd like.

In a large nonstick skillet over medium-high heat, warm the remaining 2 Tbsp olive oil. Add as much of the zucchini to the pan as will fit in a single layer without crowding. You may need to work in batches, depending on the size of your skillet; you're looking for sautéed zucchini, not steamed zucchini. Sprinkle with a generous pinch of salt and cook, stirring now and then, until just softened and browned in spots, 8 to 10 minutes. Transfer the zucchini to a serving platter. If working in batches, keep the first batch warm and repeat with the remaining zucchini, adding more oil to the skillet if needed.

Drizzle the zucchini with the reserved dressing. Serve warm or at room temperature.

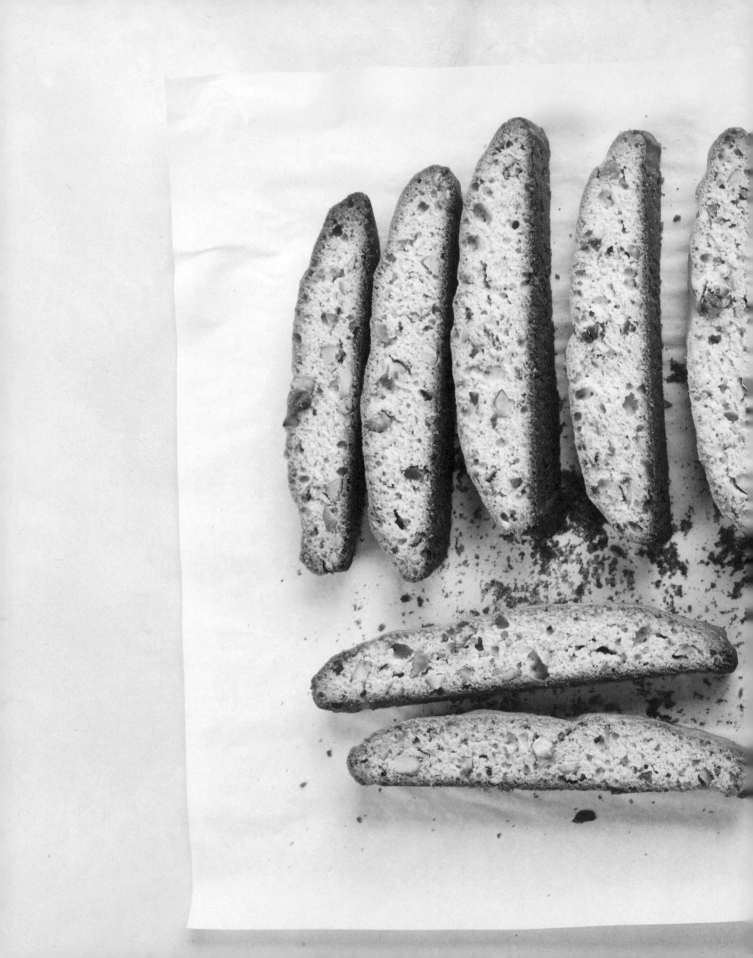

Pistachio Mandelbrot Cookies

MAKES 12 COOKIES

A close cousin of Italian biscotti, *mandelbrot* is a traditional almond-flavored Ashkenazi cookie (*mandel* means "almond" and *brot* means "bread"). These cookies are one of my grandmother's specialties. She typically makes a vanilla-and-chocolate version that doesn't include nuts. She divides the dough into thirds, mixes cocoa powder into one portion, and then sandwiches that portion between the other two portions to make vanilla cookies with chocolate centers. I've opted for a simpler version that includes chopped pistachios (because I love them and because they fit the green theme).

2 eggs

½ cup [100 g] sugar

¼ cup [60 ml] vegetable oil

1 tsp vanilla extract

1 tsp almond extract

1 tsp baking powder

1 tsp kosher salt

1½ cups [180 g] all-purpose flour

½ cup [70 g] shelled pistachios, roughly chopped

Preheat your oven to 350°F [180°C]. Line a sheet pan with parchment paper.

In a large bowl, whisk together the eggs, sugar, oil, and vanilla and almond extracts, mixing well. Add the baking powder and salt and whisk well to make sure they are thoroughly incorporated. Stir in the flour and then fold in the nuts. The dough will be sticky, almost more of an extremely thick batter.

Use a rubber spatula to scrape the dough onto the prepared sheet pan. Wet your hands (to prevent the dough from sticking to them) and use them to shape the dough into an 8-by-5-in [20-by-12-cm] rectangle.

Bake the loaf until it is golden brown and firm to the touch, about 30 minutes. Remove from the oven and carefully transfer the loaf to a cutting board (you can let it cool down a bit first if you'd like, but I am impatient). Use a serrated knife to cut the loaf into 12 cookies, each about ¾ in [2 cm] thick. I always trim off the ends and snack on them and I highly suggest it. No one needs to know.

Lay the cookies on one of their cut sides on the still-warm sheet pan and return them to the oven. Bake until the exposed sides are dried out a bit, about 5 minutes. Carefully turn each cookie over and bake until the second sides are also dried out a bit, another 5 minutes. Transfer the cookies to a wire rack to cool (they will crisp as they cool).

Serve at room temperature. Leftover cookies can be stored in a tightly covered container at room temperature for up to 3 days.

It's Me Again

DOUG'S FISH SALAD

Leftover striped bass can be turned into my dad's delicious fish salad. Remove and discard any fish skin and then flake the fish into a large bowl. For each serving, add a chopped hard-boiled egg, a little minced onion (any color), and about ½ stalk finely diced celery. Bind with however much mayonnaise you like and season with prepared white horseradish, salt, and pepper. Serve on toasted English muffins or any kind of toast or with crackers. If you're living a low-carb lifestyle, this is also great on cucumber slices or wrapped in lettuce.

ZUCCHINI HUMMUS

Place leftover zucchini, green goddess and all, into a food processor with a drained and rinsed can of chickpeas. Purée until smooth and season to taste with tahini, lemon juice, and salt. Serve with warm pita bread (or crispy pita chips) or crunchy vegetables for dipping. It's also good as a neighbor to roasted chicken, grilled shrimp, or even scrambled eggs.

PEA VICHYSSOISE

Leftover Crushed Potatoes + Peas can be turned into a green version of the classic potato-and-leek soup. Start by finely chopping a large leek and then putting it into a big bowl of water and swishing it around to get all of the dirt to drop to the bottom of the bowl. Lift the chopped leek out with your hands and add it to a large pot in which you've already melted a knob of butter. Cook over medium heat until the leek is nice and soft and melty. Add whatever potatoes and peas remain and enough vegetable stock to barely cover the vegetables. Bring to a simmer and cook, stirring to break up the potatoes, until the soup is warm and thick. Purée with an immersion blender or in a countertop blender. If you want it to be perfectly smooth, pass it through a sieve. Season to taste with salt and serve hot, or let cool to room temperature, cover, refrigerate until chilled, and serve cold (which is traditional for vichyssoise). Whatever temperature you serve it at, top it with a dollop of sour cream or crème fraîche and a few turns from a pepper mill.

Grace's Birthday Late Lunch

VIRGINIA PEANUTS

MUSTARDY DEVILED EGGS

SIMPLEST PULLED PORK WITH VINEGAR SLAW

SWEET POTATO OVEN FRIES WITH COMEBACK SAUCE

PICKLED SPRING VEGETABLES

HEALTHY, HAPPY WIFE CAKE

Grace's birthday falls in early June and putting together a late-afternoon lunch is one way I love to celebrate my favorite person. This menu takes inspiration from Grace's Virginia upbringing, and because Grace has type 1 diabetes, it is also not-too-obviously low in carbohydrates. It's always important to me that she can enjoy everything on our table, *especially* on her birthday. I don't love putting out lots of snacks before a meal, but for a long, lingering lunch, I like having a few things to nosh with drinks. This menu starts with a big bowl of Virginia peanuts because there's no need to fuss with something that's already great (plus Grace's folks often bring us a big tin when they visit). Deviled eggs, heavy on the mustard, go near the peanuts, and then, after a little while, I sneak into the kitchen to pull the pork and sweet potatoes out of the oven and the slaw and pickles out of the fridge. It's an easy meal to prepare and even easier to eat, and just when everyone says they can't make room for another thing, I bring in the cake and watch everyone magically create just a little more space. This one is for you, darling.

UP TO 3 DAYS AHEAD

Make the pickled vegetables and store in a covered container in the refrigerator.

Cut the sweet potatoes into fries, shred the cabbage for the slaw, and wrap in ever-so-damp paper towels. Store in separate plastic bags in the refrigerator. Make the comeback sauce and store in a covered container in the refrigerator.

Make the pork and store in an airtight container in the refrigerator.

Cook the eggs for the deviled eggs. Let them cool to room temperature, then store unpeeled in the refrigerator.

UP TO 1 DAY AHEAD

Make the cake (frost it and everything), cover, and store in the refrigerator. Make the slaw and store, covered, in the refrigerator.

UP TO A FEW HOURS AHEAD

Make the deviled eggs and cover with plastic wrap or a damp paper towel and store in the refrigerator.

Take the cake out of the refrigerator if you prefer it at room temperature (I love it cold, but whatever works for you!).

LAST MOMENT

Put out the eggs and peanuts for guests while you roast the sweet potatoes and put the pork into a baking dish in a 300°F [150°C] oven until warm, about 15 minutes.

Mustardy Deviled Eggs

MAKES 12

When I was in college in Manhattan, I studied poetry for a couple of semesters with the poet Karen Swenson. I remember her fearlessness and independence so clearly. She would travel alone for months at a time across continents and write about her experiences. She loved to entertain and had a Rolodex of interesting New Yorkers to call on. Since all of my poems were about food, she knew I loved to cook, and I started helping her out with her dinner parties every now and then in exchange for getting to sit at a table filled with interesting people. She always said a party wasn't a party without deviled eggs. I couldn't agree more. I especially like these, which are as heavy on the mustard as they are on mayonnaise.

6 eggs

3 Tbsp mayonnaise

1 Tbsp Dijon mustard

1 Tbsp whole-grain mustard

1 Tbsp fresh lemon juice

Few dashes of hot sauce

¼ tsp kosher salt, plus more as needed

A small handful of finely chopped fresh chives or Italian parsley leaves (a little bit of parsley stem is fine!)

Put the eggs into a medium saucepan and add water to cover by 1 in [2.5 cm]. Set the pan over high heat and bring the water to a boil. The moment it comes to a full boil, turn off the heat, cover the pot, and set a timer for 10 minutes. Meanwhile, prepare a large bowl of ice water.

When the timer rings, transfer the eggs to the ice water. Once the eggs are cool enough to handle, peel them. If you are having trouble peeling them cleanly (it happens, especially if your eggs are very fresh), place them, one at a time, in a clean jelly jar with about 3 Tbsp water, screw on the lid tightly, and shake the jar like mad. The shell should come off much more easily.

Cut each egg in half lengthwise, carefully remove the yolks from the whites, and reserve the whites. Put the yolks into a food processor, add the mayonnaise, both mustards, the lemon juice, hot sauce, and salt and purée until smooth (you can instead do this in a bowl with a fork, but it won't be quite as smooth). Season to taste with a bit more salt if needed.

Use a small spoon to fill the egg whites with the yolk mixture. Sprinkle with the chives and serve immediately.

Simplest Pulled Pork with Vinegar Slaw

SERVES 6

When Grace and I drive to Virginia Beach to visit her family, we sometimes take the long way to stop for pulled pork at Pierce's Pitt Bar-B-Que in Williamsburg, where Grace often went when she was in college, or head to Doumar's in Norfolk for minced pork and slaw sandwiches. I've come to love these pit stops and now truly understand that one of the benefits of marriage is getting a whole new set of nostalgic foods. If you prefer to enjoy this pork and slaw as a sandwich, just serve them on soft rolls.

One 3-lb [1.4-kg] boneless pork shoulder roast (cuts labeled Boston butt and pork butt will work, too)

Kosher salt

1½ tsp freshly ground black pepper

⅓ cup [80 ml] water

1 lb [455 g] green cabbage, cored and thinly sliced (about ⅓ small head)

½ cup [120 ml] apple cider vinegar

½ tsp red pepper flakes

3 Tbsp yellow or Dijon mustard

Preheat your oven to 275°F [135°C].

Sprinkle the pork all over with 2 tsp salt and the pepper and rub them in well with your hands. Put the pork into a Dutch oven or large baking dish and pour the water around (not on) the meat. Cover tightly with a lid or aluminum foil.

Place the pork in the oven and cook, turning it every 2 hours (and remembering to cover it after you turn it), until it's incredibly tender when tested with a fork and shreds easily, 5 to 6 hours.

Meanwhile, put the cabbage into a large bowl, add ¼ cup [60 ml] of the vinegar, and sprinkle with the red pepper flakes and 1 tsp kosher salt. Use your hands to scrunch everything together so the cabbage softens slightly. This can hang at room temperature for a few hours or in the refrigerator for longer.

Use tongs or two forks to shred the pork. Discard any large pieces of fat as you work. Stir the mustard and the remaining ¼ cup [60 ml] vinegar into the pork and its cooking liquid, sort of really whipping it all together to make sure the seasonings get well incorporated. Season the pork to taste with salt.

Serve the pork warm with the slaw alongside.

Sweet Potato Oven Fries with Comeback Sauce

SERVES 6

The spice mixture on these sweet potatoes gives them a sort of seasoned-fry effect (the power of garlic powder!). The cayenne gives them a little zip, and if you really like heat, you can double or even triple the amount (or if you don't like heat, just leave it out). Comeback sauce, a mixture that resembles both rémoulade and Russian dressing, hails from central Mississippi and gets its name from the fact that it's so good it'll make you come back for more. I love its name and story as much as I love dipping fries into it.

1 tsp kosher salt, plus a pinch

1 tsp garlic powder

1 tsp sweet paprika

1 tsp ground cayenne pepper

¼ cup [60 ml] olive oil

2 lb [910 g] sweet potatoes (about 3 large), scrubbed and cut into fries ⅓ in [8 mm] thick

¼ cup [60 g] mayonnaise

1 Tbsp ketchup

2 Tbsp prepared white horseradish

2 Tbsp fresh lemon juice

Position one rack in the center of your oven and a second rack in the top third and preheat to 425°F [220°C]. At the same time, place two sheet pans in the oven to heat.

In a large bowl, stir together 1 tsp of the salt, the garlic powder, paprika, cayenne, and olive oil. Add the sweet potatoes and stir to coat well with the oil mixture (your hands are really the best tools for this job).

Once the oven and the sheet pans are hot, divide the sweet potatoes evenly between the sheet pans and spread them out in a single layer. Roast until the undersides are starting to brown and crisp, about 15 minutes. Flip the fries over, switch the pans between the racks so the sweet potatoes cook evenly, and continue to roast until completely tender when pierced with a paring knife and browned and a bit crisp all over, about another 15 minutes.

While the sweet potatoes are roasting, in a small bowl, whisk together the mayonnaise, ketchup, horseradish, and lemon juice. Season with the remaining pinch of salt and reserve.

Transfer the sweet potatoes to a serving platter and the sauce to a small bowl. Serve immediately.

Pickled Spring Vegetables

SERVES 6

Inspired by the plate of pickles Grace once enjoyed at Lantern, Andrea Reusing's restaurant in Chapel Hill, North Carolina, these vegetables are transformed by a simple brine into amplified versions of themselves. Try any combination of vegetables or just a single vegetable, or you can even make pickled peach wedges or plums (both of which would be delicious with the pork). I like to make these at least a day ahead so they have a chance to take on a nice pickled flavor (plus you can cross them off of your to-do list).

1 cup [240 ml] water

1 cup [240 ml] distilled white vinegar

2 Tbsp kosher salt

1 Tbsp sugar

2 Tbsp mixed whole spices (I like a combination of red pepper flakes, allspice berries, and fennel, coriander, cumin, and celery seeds)

2 garlic cloves, thinly sliced

1 lb [455 g] crunchy spring vegetables (such as spring onions, baby leeks, radishes, fennel, and/or asparagus), ends trimmed and cut into bite-size pieces

In a small saucepan, combine the water, vinegar, salt, sugar, spices, and garlic. Set the pan over high heat and bring the mixture to a boil, stirring to dissolve the salt and sugar. Remove from the heat and let the mixture cool down for 5 minutes; it should be nice and warm but not boiling hot.

Put the vegetables into a tall, nonreactive container in which they fit snugly. Pour the warm brine over the vegetables (if they aren't quite covered, add a splash of water). Cover the container tightly and give it a shake to help distribute everything evenly.

Let the container sit until it reaches room temperature and then either serve the pickled vegetables immediately or store them in the fridge for up to 3 days (if you end up storing them, give the container a shake every now and then).

Healthy, Happy Wife Cake

SERVES 8

The Happy Wife, Happy Life Cake in *Small Victories*, my first cookbook, was as much a simple cake recipe as it was a love letter to my wife. Seeing the recipe take on its own life in other peoples' families and kitchens has been one of my most gratifying experiences as a cookbook author (and, real talk, as an out and proud gay woman). As these things go, though, life changed quite a bit between the time I wrote that recipe and when the book came out. During the interim, Grace was diagnosed with type 1 diabetes and that beloved cake became more of a memory than something we regularly eat. I set out to make a new version that would meet all of Grace's current health requirements and also be just as satisfying. After much trial and error, I landed on this recipe, which is great not only for folks with type 1, but also for anyone looking for a treat that's kinder to the body than a typical cake.

The two cakes differ in a number of ways. This version is just a single layer rather than two layers (that means fewer carbohydrates per slice, plus the cake is easier to make!), uses coconut sugar instead of granulated sugar and less of it (coconut sugar is easier for the body to regulate), calls for almond meal instead of wheat flour (which makes it lower in carbohydrates and gluten free), and includes a hefty dose of cinnamon to add nice, warm flavor where there used to be sugar. I also use dark chocolate in the frosting and make just enough frosting to cover the top of the cake with a thin layer, instead of cloaking the whole thing. Lastly, I use a ton of fresh berries instead of jam, which eliminates a lot of added sugar and adds undeniable beauty. You can skip the frosting and berries and bake the batter in a loaf pan instead of a cake pan for a chocolate-almond tea bread.

CAKE

2¼ cups [250 g] superfine almond meal

½ cup [50 g] Dutch-processed cocoa powder, sifted

2 tsp baking powder

½ tsp kosher salt

1 Tbsp ground cinnamon

6 eggs, separated

½ cup [70 g] coconut sugar

4 Tbsp [55 g] unsalted butter, melted

1 Tbsp vanilla extract

½ cup [120 ml] strong brewed coffee, at room temperature

½ tsp fresh lemon juice, distilled white vinegar, or apple cider vinegar

FROSTING

½ cup [90 g] dark chocolate chips (at least 60 percent cacao) or roughly chopped chocolate

½ cup [120 g] sour cream

TO SERVE

1½ cups [200 g] fresh berries (preferably blueberries and raspberries)

To make the cake: Preheat your oven to 350°F [180°C]. Spray the bottom and sides of an 8-in [20-cm] round cake pan with baking spray and line the bottom with a circle of parchment paper. Spray the parchment paper for good measure and set the pan aside.

In a large bowl, whisk together the almond meal, cocoa powder, baking powder, salt, and cinnamon. In a medium bowl, whisk together the egg yolks, ¼ cup [35 g] of the sugar, the butter, vanilla, and coffee. Stir the almond meal mixture into the egg mixture, mixing well. The mixture will be quite thick, almost like a paste.

Put the egg whites into a stand mixer fitted with the whisk attachment (or use a handheld electric mixer or a whisk and some elbow grease) and beat on medium-high speed until foamy, about 30 seconds. With the mixer still running on medium-high speed, slowly add the lemon juice and the remaining ¼ cup [35 g] sugar and continue beating until the egg whites billow and turn into a fluffy, almost glossy cloud of stiff peaks, about another 2 minutes. To test if the egg whites are stiff enough, lift the whisk attachment. The whites that cling to it should stand nice and tall and not droop over (that's a soft peak). If they're not quite there yet, just keep mixing until they are.

Use a rubber spatula to fold one-third of the beaten egg whites into the cake batter. It's okay if you sort of stir this one-third in rather than fold it in, as the cake batter is quite stiff and these egg whites will help lighten it. Add half of the remaining egg whites and gently and carefully fold them into the batter by cutting your spatula down through the middle of the bowl, scraping the bottom of the bowl,

and then pulling the mixture back up. Think of it like cutting in the egg whites and folding them with the batter. This helps preserve the air you worked hard to create in the egg whites. Fold in the rest of the egg whites the same way. Use the rubber spatula to scrape the batter into the prepared cake pan and then smooth the surface so it is even.

Bake the cake until it has risen, is firm to the touch, and a toothpick inserted in the center comes out with just a couple of crumbs (and not wet batter) clinging to it, 40 to 45 minutes. Let the cake cool in the pan on a wire rack to room temperature.

To make the frosting: Bring a small saucepan of water to a boil and then lower the heat to a simmer. Put the chocolate chips into a medium heatproof bowl and set it over the saucepan (make sure the bowl doesn't touch the water; if it does, pour some water out). Stir the chocolate until it melts and is smooth, about 2 minutes. (Alternatively, you can melt the chocolate in a microwave in 15-second intervals, stirring between the intervals.) Remove the bowl from the saucepan and whisk in the sour cream. The frosting should be smooth and quite silky.

Use a dinner knife to loosen the edges of the cake from the pan sides and then invert it onto your work surface. Peel off and discard the parchment, then invert the cake one more time onto a serving platter. Spread the frosting evenly over the top of the cake and casually but thoughtfully arrange the berries on top.

Cut into wedges and serve. Leftovers can be covered and stored in the refrigerator for up to 3 days.

It's Me Again

DEVILED EGG SALAD

I like to think of leftover deviled eggs as halfway on their journey to egg salad. Finely chop whatever deviled eggs you have left, filling and all, and put them into a bowl. Add a little minced onion (any color) and a little minced celery if you're into those things in your egg salad. Bind with as much mayonnaise as you like (since the filling already has a bit, you shouldn't need too much). Serve on toast or lettuce leaves.

CUBAN SANDWICHES

Leftover pulled pork and pickled vegetables can be turned into divine Cuban sandwiches. Spread the cut sides of Cuban sandwich rolls (or any long sandwich roll with a thin, crisp crust and a soft interior) with yellow mustard and mayonnaise. Place a slice of Swiss cheese on both cut sides and then top one half with a layer of pulled pork, a few thin slices of ham, and some of the pickled vegetables. Close the sandwiches (there should be cheese on either side of the meat and pickles). Put a knob of butter into a large skillet set over medium heat. Once it melts, place as many sandwiches as will fit in a single layer. Top the sandwiches with another heavy skillet and press down hard. Cook the sandwiches until the undersides are golden brown and crisp, about 2 minutes. Remove the sandwiches

from the skillet, melt another knob of butter, and then return the sandwiches, flipping them over, to the skillet (so what used to be the tops should now be the bottoms). Top with the second skillet again and press until the second sides are browned and crisp, about 1 more minute. Cut in half on the diagonal and serve immediately. Oh, and if you have a sandwich press, by all means use it.

SWEET POTATO BREAKFAST POTATOES

Leftover sweet potato fries can be turned into breakfast potatoes. Start by sautéing a chopped onion (red, white, yellow—whatever you have) and a chopped bell pepper (red, yellow, orange—again, whatever you have) in some butter and oil in a large skillet. Season the aromatics with salt and freshly ground black pepper and add a little minced garlic or a shake of garlic powder if you like. Once the aromatics start to soften and brown on the edges, roughly chop your leftover fries and add them to the skillet. Cook the mixture, stirring now and then, until everything has crispy edges and is piping hot, about 3 minutes. Season to taste with more salt and pepper and then add a large handful of minced fresh Italian parsley. Serve with eggs any style.

Passover Seder

AN ORANGE ON THE SEDER PLATE

BEST MATZO BALL SOUP

AUNT SHARON'S BRISKET WITH CARROTS

GOLDEN BEET + HORSERADISH RELISH

CRUNCHY ASPARAGUS SALAD WITH MARCONA ALMONDS

CHAROSET QUINOA

LAZY VANILLA SEMIFREDDO WITH HONEYED STRAWBERRIES

Passover has always been the Jewish holiday I most enjoy. With its long table laden with symbolic foods, it's a bit like Jewish Thanksgiving. It falls in the spring, lasts for days, and commemorates the Jews' exodus from Egypt and their liberation from slavery. The first two nights are celebrated with a ceremonial meal known as a Seder. At my family's Seders, like at most Seders, we start and end the meal by telling the story of Passover. Religion aside, Passover seems to me a great opportunity to reflect not only on what happens when a group of people is persecuted but also on the things—the actual things and ideas and customs—they take with them when they are forced to leave their homes. Whenever my parents host a Passover Seder, it always feels especially meaningful that we light candles in my maternal grandmother's candlesticks, two of the only objects she brought with her when she and my grandfather fled eastern Europe during the horrific pogroms.

(Continued)

UP TO 1 MONTH AHEAD	Make the chicken broth and the brisket (slice it and freeze it in its sauce). Freeze both in airtight containers. Defrost overnight in the refrigerator.
UP TO 3 DAYS AHEAD	If you didn't go the freezer route, make the chicken broth and brisket (don't slice it) and refrigerate in airtight containers. Make the beet and horseradish relish and store in an airtight container in the refrigerator. Make the semifreddo.
UP TO 1 DAY AHEAD	Slice the asparagus, wrap in ever-so-damp paper towels, and store in a plastic bag or an airtight container in the refrigerator. Make the salad dressing and store in a covered container in the refrigerator.
	Scoop the schmaltz off the top of the chicken broth and make the matzo ball mixture.
	Make the quinoa and store covered in the refrigerator. Bring to room temperature before serving.
LAST MOMENT	Warm the chicken broth and cook the matzo balls.
	Dress the asparagus salad and top with the almonds.
	Slice the brisket (unless it was sliced before freezing and defrosting) and warm it in its sauce in a 300°F [150°C] oven (it will take about a half hour to heat through).
	Take the semifreddo out of the freezer, slice it, and let the slices soften for 15 minutes before topping with the strawberries and serving.

I never knew those grandparents, but I think about them often and feel most closely connected when I get to hold things that once belonged to them and cook the same types of foods they prepared. This is when food feels almost magical to me. It can make us feel linked not just to one another but also to everyone and everything that came before us. My grandparents came to America and eventually settled in Brooklyn, where they ran a bread bakery. The only time of year it was closed was on Passover, since no leavened items are consumed during the holiday. According to my mom, Passover is when my grandfather would clean the ovens, first always stopping to kiss the bricks in gratitude.

An Orange on the Seder Plate

This is not a recipe, but I could not include a Passover Seder without telling you this story. As I mentioned, Passover is all about symbolism, and nowhere is that more apparent than the Seder plate. A Seder plate is, quite literally, a special plate that is divided into different compartments for all of the symbolic foods we mention and eat during the storytelling part of the Seder. From the fresh horseradish that's meant to evoke the bitterness of slavery to the *charoset* (a paste made of apples, wine, and nuts that's actually quite delicious) that represents the mortar the Jews used to lay bricks, it's a fully loaded plate to say the least. Until he left this world, my paternal grandfather always led our family Seders, and one year he stuck an orange right in the middle of the Seder plate. He had heard an urban legend popular in many reform Jewish homes about a conservative man who had said that a woman belongs on the bimah (the platform in a synagogue from which the services are led and the Torah is read) as much as an orange belongs on a Seder plate. I was about twelve when my grandfather added this new addition to our holiday. It was encouraging to learn that not only was he my grandfather, he was also a feminist.

Best Matzo Ball Soup

SERVES 8

My late, very-great-aunt Renee taught me to make chicken soup, the one that's on the cover of *Small Victories* and the one that's unequivocally my favorite food in the whole world. The broth here is lifted from that soup and the matzo balls are based on the exact ones Aunt Renee talked me through on the phone so many times when I was a teenager with a notepad at my side. The key here is to make the broth the day before. Not only does the broth taste better a day after it's made, but the schmaltz (the chicken fat) that hardens on top is required for the best matzo balls. Almost like lard mixed with masa for a tamale, the schmaltz gives matzo balls that extra something. I toast the matzo meal directly in the schmaltz to give the final matzo balls a rich, nutty flavor. It's important to cook the matzo balls in a separate pot of water instead of directly in the soup so they don't cloud the broth, which should be, as Aunt Renee would always tell me, "as clear as crystal." While I love the simplicity of just great broth and matzo balls, especially since the soup is part of such a big meal, if you'd like it to be a bit more substantial, add 3 or 4 bone-in, skin-on chicken breasts to the broth after it has simmered for 2 hours (so the breasts cook for the last hour) and then shred the meat (discard the skin and bones) and add it back to the broth.

2½ lb [1.2 kg] chicken back-bones, necks, and/or wings

2 yellow onions, unpeeled, roughly chopped

4 celery stalks, roughly chopped

4 carrots, unpeeled, roughly chopped

1 head garlic, halved horizon-tally so the cloves are exposed

A large handful of fresh Italian parsley sprigs, stems reserved and leaves finely chopped

1 Tbsp black peppercorns

Kosher salt

3 qt [2.8 L] water

1 cup [120 g] matzo meal

4 eggs

¼ cup [60 ml] seltzer

Put the chicken pieces, onions, celery, carrots, garlic, parsley stems, peppercorns, and 1 Tbsp salt into the largest pot you have. Add the water and set the pot over high heat (if your pot is not large enough to hold all of the liquid, add as much as it can hold and then add the rest after you strain the broth). Bring to a boil and then lower the heat to a simmer. Cook the broth, stirring it every so often and skimming off and discarding any foam that rises to the top, until everything in the pot has given up all of its structural integrity and the broth is a rich golden color, about 3 hours.

Ladle the broth through a fine-mesh sieve into containers. Discard the contents of the sieve (everything in it will have given all it can by this point). Let the broth cool to room temperature and then refrigerate for at least 12 hours or up to 3 days (or freeze for up to a month and defrost overnight in the refrigerator).

Once the broth is nice and cold, a thin layer of fat will have formed on the surface. Lift the fat off with a spoon, then measure ¼ cup [50 g] of it into a medium skillet (any extra fat can be stored in a tightly capped jar in the refrigerator for up to 1 month and is delicious for roasting vegetables, especially potatoes). Set the skillet over medium-high heat, and, once the fat has melted, add the matzo meal and cook, stirring, until it smells nutty and is golden brown, about 1½ minutes. Transfer the mixture to a large bowl, sprinkle with 2 tsp salt, and let cool to room temperature.

Add the eggs, seltzer, and half of the chopped parsley to the cooled matzo mixture. Whisk until everything is thoroughly combined. The mixture will look loose and you might be tempted to add more matzo meal, but please don't. That's how you end up with baseballs, not matzo balls. Cover the bowl and refrigerate until the matzo meal absorbs the liquid and the mixture is nice and firm, at least 45 minutes (but you can make this mixture up to a day in advance).

When you're ready to eat, bring a large pot of water to a boil and season it generously with salt (as if you were going to cook pasta).

Wet your hands and then scoop the matzo meal mixture into sixteen uniform golf ball–size balls. Gently place the matzo balls in the boiling water and reduce the heat so the water is at a gentle simmer. The balls will sink at first and then quite quickly float to the top. Cover the pot and simmer the matzo balls until they are cooked through and start to sink back to the bottom of the pot (that's how you know they're done), about 30 minutes.

Meanwhile, warm the broth in a separate pot and season to taste with salt.

To serve, divide the matzo balls evenly among eight soup bowls and ladle the hot broth on top. Sprinkle each serving with some of the remaining chopped parsley and serve immediately.

Aunt Sharon's Brisket with Carrots

SERVES 8 AS PART OF A BIG MEAL, OR 6 IF THIS IS THE STAR OF THE SHOW

My aunt Sharon, whom I adore, hosts our entire family for a Seder every year and we all look forward to her brisket. She makes her brisket with a bottle of Heinz Chili Sauce, but I swap that out in favor of tomato paste, which is more readily available. Growing up, I didn't know brisket was something that could be prepared any other way than this. In fact, the first time I had real-deal Texas barbecue, I remember thinking, "Wow, they don't know a thing about *real* brisket!" Ha! This is best made at least the day before and then sliced and warmed before serving. It's one of those things that just tastes better reheated the next day. See timeline for make-ahead directions.

3 lb [1.4 kg] brisket, trimmed of excess fat and patted dry with paper towels (it's okay if you use more than a single piece), preferably first cut

Kosher salt

1½ cups [360 ml] water

One 6-oz [170-g] can tomato paste

1 tsp ground allspice

1 Tbsp sweet paprika

2 tsp red chile powder

4 garlic cloves, minced

2 small yellow onions or 1 large Spanish onion, halved then thinly sliced into half-moons

6 carrots, peeled and relatively thinly sliced on the diagonal

2 Tbsp apple cider vinegar

Preheat your oven to 300°F [150°C].

Season the brisket aggressively on both sides with salt. In a medium bowl, whisk together the water, tomato paste, allspice, paprika, chile powder, garlic, and 1 tsp salt. Transfer the mixture to a roasting pan large enough to comfortably accommodate the brisket.

Add the onions to the tomato paste mixture and mix well. Place the brisket on top of the mixture and spoon some of the onion mixture on top of the brisket and then top the brisket with carrots. Cover the roasting pan tightly with aluminum foil.

Bake the brisket until incredibly tender, 4 hours (flip it halfway through).

Transfer the brisket to a cutting board and thinly slice it across the grain. Stir the vinegar into the carrot mixture and then season to taste with salt. Transfer to a serving platter, top with the brisket, and serve warm.

Golden Beet + Horseradish Relish

MAKES ABOUT 2 CUPS [480 G]

Chopped cooked beets mixed with horseradish are a typical accompaniment to gefilte fish, a traditional Passover food. I like the mixture just as much with brisket, as it offers some heat and acid to cut through the richness. I use golden beets here because I think they're beautiful (and because I had a bunch when I was testing this recipe), but feel free to use red ones. This is also good as a sandwich condiment or served with any slow-cooked meat or roast chicken. If you mix it with an equal amount of sour cream, it's the best topping for a baked potato.

2 large golden beets, about ½ lb [230 g] each

One 6-oz [170-g] jar prepared white horseradish

2 Tbsp apple cider vinegar

1 Tbsp honey

1 tsp kosher salt

Bring a large saucepan of water to a boil over high heat and add the beets (the water should cover the beets; if it doesn't, add more). Cook the beets, turning them every so often, until they're tender (test with a paring knife), about 45 minutes (it may be a bit less or a bit longer depending on the size and age of the beets, so start testing at 30 minutes).

Drain the beets, transfer to a paper towel–lined cutting board, and use the paper towels to rub off the skins. Let the beets cool until they're easy to handle and then trim off and discard the root ends. Grate the beets on the coarsest holes of a box grater and transfer to a medium bowl.

Add the horseradish with its juice, vinegar, honey, and salt and stir to mix well. Serve at room temperature. Leftovers can be stored in an airtight container in the refrigerator for up to 1 week.

Crunchy Asparagus Salad with Marcona Almonds

SERVES 8

This simple salad is all about having something green and fresh and crunchy on the table to balance out the rich flavors of everything else. It's also a nod to spring and the newness that the season, and Passover itself, represent. To break the tough ends off of the asparagus, take one spear at a time, hold it horizontally with one end in either hand, and then bend it in half. It will naturally break in exactly the right spot. You can either do this with each spear (a great job for a kid!) or you can use that single spear as a measure for the rest of the spears in the bunch and cut off the tough ends in one go with a knife. Marcona almonds are wonderfully rich almonds from Spain that I am a little addicted to because of their extraordinary flavor, but they could easily be swapped out for roasted almonds, shelled pistachios, or blanched hazelnuts (all salted or unsalted, up to you). You just want some crunch in there.

3 Tbsp fresh lemon juice

⅓ cup [80 ml] extra-virgin olive oil

2 tsp honey

½ tsp kosher salt

2 lb [910 g] large asparagus (about 2 bunches), tough ends snapped off and discarded and then spears very thinly sliced on the diagonal

½ cup [70 g] Marcona almonds, roughly chopped

In a large bowl, whisk together the lemon juice, olive oil, honey, and salt. Add the asparagus to the bowl and gently combine with the dressing (I use my hands for this). Transfer to a serving platter, sprinkle with the almonds, and serve immediately.

Charoset Quinoa

SERVES 8

This quinoa side dish has all of the flavors of *charoset*, the mixture of apples, wine, and nuts that is a traditional part of the Seder plate (see "An Orange on the Seder Plate," page 165). It's especially perfect for Passover since it doesn't include anything leavened. I also love it because you can serve it at room temperature, which means you can absolutely make it in advance.

2 cups [360 g] quinoa

Kosher salt

¼ cup [60 ml] apple cider vinegar

¼ cup [60 ml] dry red wine

1 tsp ground cinnamon

1 cup [140 g] raisins

2 crisp apples (such as Honeycrisp or Granny Smith), cored and finely diced

½ cup [120 ml] olive oil

1 cup [120 g] walnut halves, roughly chopped

A small handful of fresh Italian parsley leaves (a little bit of stem is fine!), finely chopped

Rinse the quinoa thoroughly in a fine-mesh sieve (this may sound like an annoying step, but don't skip it; quinoa has a natural coating that tastes soapy). Put the rinsed quinoa into a medium saucepan with 3½ cups [840 ml] water and 2 tsp salt. Bring to a boil, then lower the heat, cover, and simmer until the quinoa has absorbed all of the water, softened, and each grain has "spiraled," about 12 minutes.

Transfer the quinoa to a large sheet pan and use a spoon to spread it out. Let cool to room temperature, then transfer to a large bowl and set aside.

Meanwhile, in a small saucepan over high heat, combine the vinegar, wine, and cinnamon and bring to a boil. Remove from the heat, add the raisins, apples, and a large pinch of salt and stir well to combine. Cover and let the mixture sit until it cools to room temperature.

Next, in a medium skillet over medium-high heat, warm the olive oil. Add the walnuts and a large pinch of salt and cook, stirring frequently, until the nuts are dark brown, about 2 minutes. Remove from the heat.

Transfer the raisins and apples and their liquid, the walnuts and all of their fragrant oil, and the parsley to the quinoa and stir well. Season the mixture to taste with salt. Serve the quinoa immediately or cover and refrigerate for up to 1 day before serving (bring to room temperature, then taste and adjust with salt if needed).

Lazy Vanilla Semifreddo with Honeyed Strawberries

SERVES 8

Since leavened items aren't permitted during Passover, typical Passover cakes and cookies tend to taste like really dense versions of their normally leavened selves. I like to veer atypical and forgo baking something all together, opting instead to serve this semifreddo (if you feel like baking, the flourless Black Forest Cake on page 108 is an excellent option). *Semifreddo*, which means "semifrozen," is a traditional Italian custard-based dessert. Instead of starting with homemade custard, I just go ahead and start with slightly melted ice cream and lighten the texture with whipped cream. I then put the mixture into the freezer for a little while until it sets up, so I can slice it and top it with strawberries sweetened with honey (any berry or stone fruit wedges would be good, too). Feel free to play around with the ice cream flavor to change the vibe here (pistachio works well). In some households, dairy for dessert on Passover isn't allowed. Although my family doesn't observe that custom, if yours does, skip the semifreddo and serve the honeyed strawberries with coconut sorbet—easy and lovely.

1½ cups [360 ml] heavy cream

1 Tbsp vanilla extract

1 pint [480 ml] vanilla ice cream, softened at room temperature until almost melted

3 cups [360 g] strawberries, hulled and thinly sliced

2 Tbsp honey

Large pinch of kosher salt

Line a 9-by-5-in [23-by-12-cm] loaf pan with plastic wrap, allowing it to hang over the sides generously.

In a stand mixer fitted with the whisk attachment, combine the cream and vanilla and beat on medium-high speed until stiff peaks form, about 3 minutes (or use a bowl and a whisk and some solid effort). Gently fold the ice cream into the whipped cream. Be sure to fold and not stir in the ice cream so you don't lose all of the air you just worked hard to create.

Use a rubber spatula to scrape the ice cream mixture into the prepared pan and then smooth the surface so it is even. Cover with the overhanging plastic wrap and freeze until just solid, at least 4 hours or up to 3 days.

To serve, invert the semifreddo onto a cutting board, peel off the plastic wrap, and cut into eight equal slices (a knife dipped in hot water and wiped dry before each cut makes easy work of this). Place the slices on individual plates and let them soften until just beginning to melt, about 15 minutes.

While the slices are softening, put the strawberries into a large bowl, drizzle with the honey, and sprinkle with the salt. Use a fork (or your hands!) to crush about one-third of the strawberries, then give the mixture a good stir. The strawberries should be slightly saucy.

Evenly divide the honeyed strawberries among the softened slices of semifreddo. Serve immediately.

It's Me Again

BRISKET PHO Leftover chicken broth and brisket can come together to make a version of *pho* that's completely unrecognizable from either leftover's previous life. Start by placing a halved white onion, a few garlic cloves, and a large piece of fresh ginger under the broiler to char slightly. Put these into a large pot with whatever broth you have left, plus a piece of kombu (dried seaweed) if you have any, a cinnamon stick, and a star anise pod. Simmer for about 30 minutes to let all of the flavors infuse. Pull out and discard the solids (or just strain the broth) and then season the broth to taste with fish sauce and soy sauce. Serve piping hot in large bowls filled with rice noodles (prepare those according to package directions) and top with thin slices of the brisket. Serve with a platter of fresh herbs (cilantro, mint, and Thai basil are all traditional), thinly sliced white onion and jalapeño chile, and bottles of fish sauce and chile sauce. This way, diners can customize their bowls as they wish.

CRISPY TOFU + ASPARAGUS STIR-FRY Pat a block of firm tofu dry with a kitchen towel and cut it into bite-size cubes. Toss them with enough cornstarch to coat lightly (about 3 Tbsp). Heat a slick of neutral oil in a large skillet over high heat and, working in batches if needed, cook the tofu in a single layer, turning as needed, until nicely browned all over, about 8 minutes. Season the tofu generously with salt and transfer to a plate. Add a bit more oil to the skillet along with some minced or grated fresh ginger and garlic. Once they sizzle, add whatever asparagus salad is left over (dressing and almonds are fine!) and cook, stirring, until the asparagus is just softened, about 2 minutes. Return the crispy tofu to the skillet and drizzle with soy sauce to taste and a splash of rice vinegar. Serve spooned over any cooked grain (rice of any color, quinoa, whatever), preferably with a fried egg on top.

Tortilla Soup for a Chilly Spring Evening

SIMPLEST + BEST NACHOS

EASIEST ALMOND HORCHATA

TORTILLA SOUP WITH THE WORKS

PINEAPPLE WITH HOMEMADE TAJÍN

One of the best meals of my life was at the house of my friends Kate Arding and Mona Talbott, who live across the river from us in the Hudson Valley. Kate and Mona run Talbott & Arding Cheese and Provisions in Hudson, New York, where they sell beautiful cheeses, prepared foods, and gorgeous baked goods in an atmosphere of overall positive energy. They invited Grace and me over after I did a book signing at their shop (where the blue gingham spine of *Small Victories* matched everything). It was one of those meals where the four of us quickly turned into nearly twenty of us.

Mona did not break a sweat. She had made a huge pot of chicken soup with plenty of chiles the day before and then, in her words, "raided the store" and put out bowls of wonderful things to stir into the soup. There were heaps of radishes and fresh cilantro, tons of limes and more chiles, and plenty of crispy tortillas. Kate and Mona put out stacks of bowls, a pile of spoons, and that was that. We all filled our bowls with the fragrant broth and went shopping for toppings. It was simple and easygoing—and indelibly memorable. This menu is an homage to that evening, to good friends and supportive communities, and to two really hardworking, easy-laughing women.

UP TO 1 MONTH AHEAD	Make the soup (minus the toppings), let it cool to room temperature, and then freeze in airtight containers. Defrost in the refrigerator overnight before warming in a pot on the stove.
UP TO 3 DAYS AHEAD	If you didn't go the freezer route, make the soup (minus the toppings), let it cool to room temperature, and then refrigerate in airtight containers.
UP TO 1 DAY AHEAD	Make the *horchata* and store in a covered container in the refrigerator.
UP TO A FEW HOURS AHEAD	Make the *tajín* and slice the pineapple (just cover it and leave it at room temperature).
LAST MOMENT	Make and serve the nachos. Pour everyone some horchata. Warm the soup while you crisp the tortillas and set out the rest of the toppings. Set out the pineapple.

Simplest + Best Nachos

SERVES 8

These nachos are an excellent example of the power of simplicity. Crispy chips are draped with a great, easy cheese sauce and finished with a little sprinkle of cilantro and that is that. Some things are best left alone. If you'd like a bit more flair, these nachos are also good topped with pickled jalapeños (or you can finely chop a large handful of them and add it to the cheese sauce). The cheese sauce can also go on cooked elbow noodles to create delicious macaroni and cheese (put the dressed noodles into a baking dish, sprinkle more cheese and some bread crumbs on top, and bake until crisp and bubbling). Or try spooning the sauce on steamed or roasted broccoli or cauliflower. Yum. Buy top-quality chips, preferably ones that aren't too thin so they will hold up well under the sauce, or make your own by quartering round corn tortillas and frying them in a large, heavy pot filled with 1 in [2.5 cm] neutral oil.

1 Tbsp unsalted butter

1 Tbsp all-purpose flour

1/2 cup [120 ml] whole milk

3/4 cup [75 g] coarsely grated sharp Monterey Jack cheese

1/2 cup [50 g] coarsely grated mild Cheddar cheese

1/4 tsp kosher salt

2 tsp hot sauce (preferably Cholula brand)

One 13-oz [370-g] bag best tortilla chips you can find

A large handful of fresh cilantro leaves (a little bit of stem is fine!), roughly chopped

In a small saucepan over medium heat, melt the butter. Add the flour and cook, stirring, until light golden brown, about 45 seconds. While stirring constantly, slowly pour in the milk to create a smooth sauce (make sure you scrape the sides and bottom of the pot). If little bits of flour turn into lumps, don't sweat it, as they'll dissolve once the cheeses are added. Continue to cook, stirring now and then, until the mixture begins to thicken, about 1½ minutes. Add both of the cheeses, the salt, and the hot sauce and mix well. Cook just until the cheeses melt, about 2 minutes, stirring continually to make sure the sauce is supersmooth. Turn the heat as low as it goes to keep the sauce warm.

Put a single, even layer of tortilla chips on a serving platter, drizzle with some of the cheese sauce, and sprinkle with a little of the cilantro. Repeat the layers until you've used up all of your chips, cheese sauce, and cilantro. Serve *immediately*. Cheese sauce waits for no one.

Easiest Almond Horchata

SERVES 8

Horchata, a popular cinnamon-flavored Mexican beverage usually made with soaked and ground rice and sometimes nuts and seeds, beautifully rides the line between sweet and savory. This almond version starts with almond meal, which means you don't have to soak and grind anything and you'll have creamy almond horchata quickly. I love serving it with the tortilla soup because it tames the soup's heat (both temperature and spice). To make this an adult beverage, spike each glass with a little light or dark rum (about 2 Tbsp per drink is good). Any leftover sweetened condensed milk should be held on to and thought of as an excuse for Vietnamese Iced Coffee (page 211).

4 cups [960 ml] whole milk

½ cup [55 g] superfine almond meal

½ tsp ground cinnamon

½ tsp kosher salt

⅛ tsp almond extract

1½ tsp vanilla extract

7 oz [200 g] sweetened condensed milk (one-half of a standard can)

3 cups [720 ml] water

Ice cubes for serving

In a large bowl, whisk together the whole milk, almond meal, cinnamon, salt, almond and vanilla extracts, and sweetened condensed milk. Transfer the mixture to a covered container and refrigerate for at least 30 minutes or up to 24 hours. This will allow the almond and cinnamon flavors to infuse the milk.

Shake the container to give everything a good mix and then transfer the mixture to a large pitcher. I like the tiny bits of almond so I leave them in, but if you prefer a smoother drink, strain it through a fine-mesh sieve into the pitcher. Whisk the water into the mixture to dilute it.

Fill eight glasses with ice and divide the horchata evenly among them. Serve immediately.

Tortilla Soup with The Works

SERVES 8

Like most soups, this is best if you make it the day before (it always tastes better, plus your main task is done before your friends even arrive). You'll need to wait until not long before serving to crisp the tortillas, however. On a spice scale of one to ten (with ten being an instant sweat), this soup is about a seven. The warming heat comes from canned chipotles (smoked jalapeños that come packed in a rich sauce called *adobo*; cans are widely available in large grocery stores). If you prefer less heat, just add one or two rather than the whole can. If you can't track them down, substitute 2 Tbsp red chile powder or 2 fresh jalapeño chiles, roughly chopped (they won't give you the same depth of flavor, but they will definitely give you a kick). If you want extra chicken in the soup, add 2 large bone-in, skin-on chicken breasts to the pot when you add the whole chicken.

1 large chicken, about 4 lb [1.8 kg], quartered (see Note)

2 large yellow onions, unpeeled, quartered through the stem end

1 head garlic, halved horizontally so the cloves are exposed

One 28-oz [794-g] can crushed tomatoes

One 7-oz [200-g] can chipotle chiles in adobo sauce

1 large bunch fresh cilantro, tough stems and leaves separated

12 cups [2.8 L] water

Kosher salt

Twelve 6-in [15-cm] corn tortillas

Canola or other neutral oil for frying

Sour cream, lime wedges, thinly sliced white onion, thinly sliced radishes, and thinly sliced red or green cabbage for serving

Put the chicken, yellow onions, garlic, tomatoes, chipotles with their sauce, and the tough cilantro stems into the largest pot you have. Add the water and 2 Tbsp salt. (If your pot is not large enough to hold all of the water, add whatever water fits now and add the rest after you strain the broth.) Bring to a boil over high heat, then lower the heat to a simmer and cook, stirring every so often and skimming off and discarding any foam that rises to the top, until everything in the pot has given up all of its structural integrity and the broth is wonderfully fragrant, at least 2 hours and preferably 3 hours.

Use tongs to retrieve the chicken pieces, place them in a large bowl or on a sheet pan, and let sit until they're cool enough to handle. Strain the broth through a colander into a clean pot (discard the contents of the colander). A few bits of onion might end up going through the holes of the colander, but that's not the end of the world. This isn't a refined consommé.

Once the chicken is cool enough to handle, remove and discard the skin and bones, tear all of the meat into bite-size pieces, and add them to the broth. Season the soup to taste with salt and keep it warm over low heat.

Once the soup is over low heat, cut the tortillas into strips ½ in [12 mm] wide. Pour the oil to a depth of 1 in [2.5 cm] into a large, heavy pot over high heat. While the oil heats, line a sheet pan with paper towels and place it near the stove. The oil is ready when a tortilla strip dropped into it sizzles on contact. Add a large handful of tortilla strips and fry, stirring with a spider (check out page 284), tongs, or a slotted spoon, until crisp and golden brown, about 1½ minutes. Transfer to the towel-lined sheet pan and sprinkle with a generous pinch of salt. Repeat the process until all of the tortilla strips are fried. Make sure to regulate the heat while frying so the tortillas don't burn.

To serve, put the crispy tortilla strips and reserved cilantro leaves into separate bowls alongside bowls of sour cream, lime wedges, white onion, radishes, and cabbage. Set these bowls up somewhere close to your pot of soup. Let your guests build their own bowls, topping them as they like. Some people like to put the tortillas on the bottom of the bowl so they soften almost as if they were noodles, while others prefer to put them on top so they stay crisp. I say, why choose?

Note: To quarter a chicken, pull its legs apart so you can get to the thigh joints, then cut through those joints with a sturdy chef's knife. You want to remove the left drumstick and thigh in one piece and the right drumstick and thigh in another whole piece (I have no idea which is left and which is right, but it really doesn't matter). Use sturdy kitchen scissors or your chef's knife to help you separate the backbone from the breasts and wings. Throw the backbone into the soup pot (so much flavor!). Use your knife to assertively cut the breasts apart through the breastbone and throw them, with their wings attached, into the soup pot, too. You can, of course, just put the whole chicken into the pot, but these chicken pieces are much easier to maneuver and somehow seem to take up less space. Up to you!

Pineapple with Homemade Tajín

SERVES 8

Tajín is a ground Mexican seasoning made of dried red chile, salt, and dehydrated lime juice. When I can't find a bottle or I run out of it, I like to make my own. For the chile, I use fruity *gochugaru* (Korean red pepper flakes) or smoky Urfa pepper (from Turkey), but any coarse red pepper flakes or even regular old red chile powder will work. Combined with salt and tart lime zest and sprinkled on sweet pineapple, you basically get every single flavor in one bite and a wonderful end to a rich meal.

1 Tbsp coarse red pepper flakes or red chile powder

1 tsp kosher salt

Finely grated zest and juice of 1 lime, separated

2 ripe pineapples, peeled, cored, cut into bite-size pieces

In a small bowl, stir together the red pepper flakes, salt, and lime zest. Place the pineapple on a serving platter and drizzle with the lime juice. Sprinkle with the tajín and serve immediately.

It's Me Again

PINEAPPLE SALSA

Leftover Pineapple with Homemade Tajín begs to be salsa. Finely dice whatever pineapple you have left (or blitz it in the food processor). For every handful of pineapple, add about ½ jalapeño chile that you've finely minced (or less or more depending on your spice tolerance), plus a small handful of roughly chopped fresh cilantro leaves, about 1 Tbsp minced red onion, and the juice of about ½ juicy lime. Season to taste with salt and let the mixture sit for at least 10 minutes before serving to allow the flavors to blend. This is delicious on grilled fish or chicken, as a dip for tortilla chips, spooned over avocado slices, or tucked into pork tacos. If you really want to go to town, make sure the pork in those tacos is the Simplest Pulled Pork with Vinegar Slaw (page 153). And please call me so I can swing by because that's going to be a fun and great meal!

ARROZ CON POLLO

For every 3 cups [720 ml] of leftover Tortilla Soup, add ¾ cup [150 g] long-grain rice. Cover and simmer over low heat until the rice is tender, about 20 minutes. Add a handful of frozen peas, stir them in, turn off the heat, cover, and let sit for 10 minutes for the rice to absorb more liquid and for the peas to cook through. Sprinkle with cilantro. This is really nice with a simple salad of sliced avocado and white onion dressed with olive oil and lime juice.

SPICY POZOLE

Leftover Tortilla Soup can be turned into the most wonderful pozole. Heat up whatever soup you have left and add whatever sliced onion and cabbage you have left from the toppings. Get a can of hominy (check out the aisle of the grocery store that stocks Tex-Mex ingredients, as it's often near the pickled jalapeños). Drain the hominy, rinse it, and add as much to the soup as you like (some like a few pieces here and there and others prefer it to be more like hominy with some broth). Simmer until the cabbage and onions are softened and the hominy and broth are piping hot, about 15 minutes. Add as much hot sauce as you like to increase the heat and/or top with thin jalapeño slices. Serve topped with any roughly chopped leftover cilantro and with any leftover lime wedges for squeezing into each bowl.

Just My Type of Dinner

CONFETTI MEATLOAF

CREAMY GARLIC MASHED CAULIFLOWER

BUTTER LETTUCE WITH SHALLOT VINAIGRETTE

RASPBERRIES WITH COCOA WHIPPED CREAM

Grace was diagnosed with type 1 diabetes about a year after we moved into our home. Her diagnosis brought a lot of changes with it, and our kitchen became ground zero for many of them. We both committed to becoming informed about her health and to implementing whatever changes were needed to guarantee that it was supported. It turned out that many of these changes improved my health, too. As the resident worrier of our family, I figured it was harder to resist the things that tempt both of us (the same things that raise Grace's blood sugar levels and require her to take extra insulin shots) than to simply eliminate them. So we said good-bye to a lot of things we used to keep in our kitchen (I'm talking empty carbohydrates and hidden sugar) and filled the space they left with only healthy choices. That change made it impossible to make an unhealthy choice in our home.

All of that work upfront meant every decision that followed was a lot easier. We rarely even make grocery lists now. We just know to fill our baskets with tons of produce, eggs, and a bit of chicken or ground turkey or other lean protein (plus ice cream for me and a few dark chocolate bars for Grace because we're only human). It turned out that Grace's diagnosis did more than update our pantry. It also made our life together so wonderfully and calmly healthy. This meal is a good example of what we eat on a normal night at home. There is a lot of flavor, very few carbohydrates, and all my love for my amazing wife who is *just my type*.

UP TO 3 DAYS AHEAD	Make the shallot vinaigrette and store in a covered container in the refrigerator. Bring to room temperature before serving.
UP TO 1 DAY AHEAD	Wash the lettuce and store in a plastic bag or an airtight container in the refrigerator wrapped in ever-so-damp paper towels.
	Make the cauliflower and store in a covered container in the refrigerator.
	Mix the meatloaf mixture and store in a covered container in the refrigerator.
LAST MOMENT	Dress the salad, warm the cauliflower, and bake the meatloaf.
	Make the whipped cream and enjoy this easy dessert!

Confetti Meatloaf

SERVES 2 VERY HUNGRY PEOPLE AND 4 MORE SENSIBLY

If you loved the Turkey + Ricotta Meatballs in *Small Victories*, you'll love this meatloaf (and vice versa!). This recipe borrows the same technique of substituting ricotta cheese for bread crumbs and eggs (which makes it much lower in carbohydrates and gluten free to boot). To keep it full of flavor and moisture, I've added sautéed peppers and onions, finely chopped herbs and sun-dried tomatoes, tons of garlic, and a kick of salty Worcestershire. This recipe can also be easily doubled, but keep in mind it will take a little longer to bake. Depending on how you shape it, add at least 20 minutes. If you are not into turkey, you can substitute ground chicken, pork, or beef.

2 tsp plus 2 Tbsp olive oil

1 large or 2 small bell peppers (any color), stemmed, seeded, and finely diced

1 small red onion, finely diced

4 garlic cloves, minced

1 tsp dried oregano

1½ tsp kosher salt

½ tsp freshly ground black pepper

1 Tbsp Worcestershire sauce

6 olive oil–packed sun-dried tomatoes, drained and minced

2 large handfuls of fresh Italian parsley and/or basil leaves (a little bit of stem is fine!), finely chopped

¾ cup [180 g] fresh whole-milk ricotta cheese

1 lb [455 g] ground turkey (preferably dark meat)

Preheat your oven to 400°F [200°C]. Line a sheet pan with parchment paper and coat the parchment with 2 tsp of the olive oil. Set the pan aside.

In a large skillet over medium-high heat, warm the remaining 2 Tbsp olive oil. Add the bell pepper and onion and cook, stirring now and then, until softened and browned on the edges, about 8 minutes. Turn off the heat, add the garlic, and stir to combine. Let the vegetables cool down for a few minutes.

Transfer the cooled vegetables to a large bowl and add the oregano, salt, pepper, Worcestershire sauce, tomatoes, parsley, and ricotta. Stir everything well to combine (this will guarantee that everything gets mixed into the meat evenly). Add the turkey to the bowl and mix everything together (your hands are the best tools for the job).

Transfer the mixture to the prepared sheet pan and shape into a loaf measuring about 10 by 4 in [25 by 10 cm] and about 1 in [2.5 cm] high. If the mixture sticks to your hands when you're doing this, just wet them lightly. Make sure to pack the meat tightly, which will help it hold together.

Bake the meatloaf until the top is nicely browned and an instant-read thermometer inserted in the center registers 165°F [74°C], 35 to 40 minutes. Let the meatloaf cool for at least 10 minutes before slicing and serving.

Creamy Garlic Mashed Cauliflower

SERVES 4

When white potatoes and foods like rice and pasta left our repertoire, I made it my personal mission to make sure we still had the comfort of comfort food even if it no longer came under a carbohydrate guise. Enter this creamy mashed cauliflower. You can use a potato masher to crush the cauliflower, but you won't get the same smooth texture that a food processor creates. Think of this mashed cauliflower as a blank canvas that takes well to all sorts of flavors. I've made it with everything from a large handful of grated cheese (Parmesan or Cheddar work well, as does crumbled goat cheese) to leeks sautéed in butter to a pinch of saffron steeped in a tiny bit of hot water. If you make this ahead, reheat it in 1-minute intervals in the microwave, stirring between the intervals to make sure it heats up evenly (or warm in a heavy saucepan on the stove top over low heat).

1½ lb [680 g] cauliflower (about 1 large head), tough stems discarded, cut into large florets

4 large garlic cloves

Kosher salt

¼ cup [60 ml] half-and-half

Freshly ground black pepper

Put the cauliflower and garlic cloves into a large pot, add water just to cover, and a large pinch of salt. Cover the pot, set over high heat, and bring to a boil. Lower the heat to a gentle simmer and continue to cook, covered, until the cauliflower is extremely tender (test with a paring knife), about 10 minutes. Drain the cauliflower and garlic in a colander and give the colander a good shake to make sure the contents are super dry.

Transfer the cauliflower and garlic to a food processor and add the half-and-half and another generous pinch of salt. Purée until smooth, scraping down the sides of the processor bowl as needed.

Taste and adjust the seasoning with salt if needed, then transfer to a serving dish. Serve hot topped with a few grinds of black pepper.

Butter Lettuce with Shallot Vinaigrette

SERVES 4

This is the salad I most often make for us. It's dressed with a classic shallot vinaigrette that's heavy on the vinegar and mustard. The pinch of dried oregano gives it the appeal of bottled Italian dressing without all of the things that are unappealing about bottled Italian dressing. Butter lettuce is my choice here, but you can use any lettuce or a mix of lettuces. Some chopped, toasted hazelnuts are also really nice on top.

1 shallot, minced

½ tsp kosher salt, plus more as needed

2 Tbsp red wine vinegar

½ tsp dried oregano

2 tsp Dijon mustard

¼ cup [60 ml] olive oil

1 large or 2 small heads butter lettuce (also known as Bibb or Boston lettuce), leaves roughly torn or left whole

Put the shallot, salt, and vinegar into a large bowl. Rub the oregano between your fingers as you drop it into the bowl. Stir everything well to combine. Let the mixture sit for a few minutes to allow the shallot to soften slightly (this is a great time to wash your lettuce if you haven't already).

Whisk the mustard into the vinegar mixture and then, while whisking, slowly drizzle in the olive oil (the shallots make whisking a little clunky, but just go with it). Season the dressing with more salt if you think it needs it (I like to taste it on a piece of lettuce). Add the lettuce to the bowl (at this point the salad can sit at room temperature for an hour or so). Use your hands to coat the lettuce with the vinaigrette. Serve immediately.

Raspberries with Cocoa Whipped Cream

SERVES 4

The deep flavors of cocoa powder and vanilla combine to make whipped cream that's more than whipped cream and just the thing to stretch a bowl of berries into more than a bowl of berries. The combination is especially nice with a little dark chocolate grated on top. When I make this dessert for Grace, I omit the honey, and you can do the same if you're avoiding sugar for any reason.

½ cup [120 ml] heavy cream

1 Tbsp honey (optional)

1 tsp vanilla extract

1 Tbsp Dutch-processed cocoa powder

Pinch of kosher salt

2 cups [240 g] raspberries

In a stand mixer fitted with the whisk attachment, combine the cream, honey (if using), vanilla, cocoa powder, and salt and beat on medium-high speed until soft peaks form, about 2 minutes (or use a bowl and a whisk and some solid effort).

Divide the cream and berries among four small bowls. Serve immediately.

It's Me Again

OPEN-FACED MEATLOAF MELTS

For me, the best part about making meatloaf is getting to make meatloaf sandwiches on crispy English muffins the next day. To make them, split and toast the muffins and spread the cut sides *generously* with mayonnaise and Dijon mustard. Place a piece of meatloaf on top of each one and drape with a slice of cheese (I like Cheddar, but use whatever you like). Run the sandwiches under the broiler or in your toaster oven. Serve on a plate or a paper towel (let's just be honest) with a jar of pickles. Best lunch.

CREAMY CAULIFLOWER + LETTUCE SOUP

Combine whatever leftover mashed cauliflower and dressed salad you have in a medium saucepan (I know that seems weird, but just stick with me; the lettuce will add body and flavor and the dressing will add just the right amount of perkiness). Add enough vegetable or chicken stock to thin the cauliflower to the consistency of a soup rather than a mash. Bring the mixture to a boil, lower the heat, and simmer just until the lettuce is wilted and soft, about 3 minutes. Purée the soup in a blender in batches as necessary and return to the pot (or use an immersion blender). If you'd like the soup extra creamy, pass it through a fine-mesh sieve. Reheat the soup, taste for seasoning, and serve immediately with something crunchy on top, like croutons, coarse bread crumbs that you've toasted in a buttered skillet, or a handful of chopped nuts (roasted almonds or hazelnuts). Instead of, or in addition to, the crunchy finish, you can top each serving with a swirl of really good extra-virgin olive oil or heavy cream and a few minced fresh chives.

LETTUCE + SPRING PEA RISOTTO

This turns leftover, probably wilted salad into an entirely new meal. For four servings, melt 3 Tbsp butter in a large, heavy pot and add 1 cup [200 g] Arborio rice (or any starchy, short-grain rice). Cook, stirring, until the rice smells nutty, about 2 minutes. Add about 1 cup [240 ml] warm chicken or vegetable stock and cook, stirring now and then, until the liquid is absorbed. Repeat until the rice is tender and creamy, about 20 to 25 minutes all together and you'll use about 4 cups [1 L] of stock. Add another 1 Tbsp butter, whatever salad you have left (chop it first), and 2 handfuls of frozen peas. Stir well to combine and cook until the peas are tender, about 1 minute. Season to taste with salt and serve immediately. Top with grated Parmesan.

Summer

GRILLED VIETNAMESE BREAKFAST

SIMPLE BACKPACK PICNIC LUNCH

AFTERNOON TACOS

FOURTH OF JULY

MIDDLE EASTERN DINNER OUTSIDE

Grilled Vietnamese Breakfast

GRILLED VIETNAMESE FLANK STEAK

FRIED EGGS

WARM GRILLED EGGPLANT + TOMATO SALAD WITH HERBS

VIETNAMESE ICED COFFEE

One of the most educational experiences I've had was working with Tom Moorman and Larry McGuire on the cookbook for Elizabeth Street Café, their restaurant in Austin, Texas.

Elizabeth Street Café is, like all restaurants I love, more than just somewhere to have a meal. It's open all day, so you can go for breakfast, lunch, dinner, or just a coffee and a pastry or a snack and a beer. It started off as a Vietnamese restaurant but soon grew to be a bona fide French bakery. That happened when they started making their own bread for *bánh mì* (Vietnamese sandwiches), which then led to croissants to go with their coffee, and so on and on. It's colorful and welcoming, full of families and locals and folks like me who are just visiting.

Working on the book also led to me learning more about Vietnamese foodways in America (particularly in Texas and New Orleans) and how food continues to be an anchor to a place even if you're not actually there. And learning the dishes was icing on the cake. My pantry was fundamentally changed, and now I can't imagine not having a bottle of fish sauce within reach or a bunch of fresh herbs at my disposal at all times. It was great to learn that successfully making Vietnamese food at home is no different from making anything else: keep it simple and fresh. This grilled breakfast menu could obviously be enjoyed at any time of day, and I give instructions throughout on how to make it if you don't have a grill.

UP TO 1 DAY AHEAD	Marinate the steak. Make the pitcher of iced coffee (don't pour over ice just yet), cover, and store in the refrigerator.
UP TO A FEW HOURS AHEAD	Make the eggplant salad (if serving at room temperature), cover, and reserve at room temperature. Or just mix the dressing, tomatoes, and herbs and add the warm eggplant later.
LAST MOMENT	Grill the steak and the eggplant (if serving the salad warm), fry the eggs, and pour the coffee over ice.

Grilled Vietnamese Flank Steak

SERVES 4

This steak gets an incredibly simple marinade that combines the salty, punchy bite of fish sauce and sweetness of sugar to provide a deeply flavorful, caramelized crust on the outside. Thinly sliced and topped with some scallions, jalapeño slices, and cilantro, this steak is not only delicious alongside fried eggs for a Vietnamese take on steak and eggs, but also good piled on tacos, served on rice with kimchi, or paired with grilled corn and a green salad for lunch or dinner. You can also turn it into a *bánh mì*: slather a toasted roll with mayonnaise and red chile paste, layer on the steak, top with thinly sliced carrots and cucumbers that have been soaked in rice vinegar, and finish with a fistful of cilantro and some thin slices of jalapeño. If you don't have an outdoor grill, you can broil the steak (using the same timing) or you can set a large cast-iron skillet over high heat, brown the steak on both sides, and then let it finish cooking in the skillet in a 400°F [200°C] oven for just a couple of minutes.

3 Tbsp fish sauce

2 Tbsp water

2 Tbsp sugar

1 lb [455 g] flank steak, at room temperature, patted dry with paper towels

3 scallions, tough roots and dark green tops trimmed off, white and light green parts thinly sliced

½ jalapeño chile, thinly sliced (discard the seeds if you like)

1 Tbsp rice vinegar

A small handful of fresh cilantro leaves (a little bit of stem is fine!), roughly chopped

In a small bowl, whisk together 2 Tbsp of the fish sauce, the water, and the sugar until the sugar dissolves. Put the steak into a large resealable plastic bag and pour in the fish sauce mixture. Move the steak around so it's covered with the mixture, squeeze all of the air out of the bag, seal the bag, and place it in the refrigerator. Let the steak marinate for at least 4 hours, or up to overnight.

Once the steak has marinated, bring it to room temperature. While it's doing that, get your outdoor grill going (gas or charcoal) with high heat and make sure the grate is superclean. If your grill needs it, brush the grate with some neutral oil (I like to fold up a paper towel and drizzle it with oil and then use tongs to rub it on the grate).

(Continued)

Remove the steak from the marinade and pat it dry with paper towels. Grill the steak, turning it once, until nicely charred on both sides and just barely firm to the touch, about 5 minutes per side (do 3 to 4 minutes if you like it rare and 6 to 7 minutes if you like it well done). Transfer the steak to a cutting board and let it rest for 10 minutes.

While the steak is resting, put the remaining 1 Tbsp fish sauce into a medium bowl along with the scallions, jalapeño, vinegar, and cilantro and stir to combine.

Thinly slice the steak across the grain and place the slices on a serving platter. Drizzle with whatever juices have accumulated on the board and top with the scallion mixture. Serve warm.

Fried Eggs

I won't give you a recipe for plain fried eggs because that seems a little boring. But because I like to eat them so much, and I am very particular about how I make them, I'll give you a quick rundown on my preferred technique (if you own *Small Victories*, it's the same technique I used for the Olive Oil–Fried Eggs with Yogurt + Lemon). Use a nonstick skillet. It's an egg's best friend. Place it over medium-high heat with just enough olive oil to barely coat the surface. Crack as many eggs into the pan as will fit in a single layer (with some space around them) and sprinkle each one with a little salt and a few grinds of black pepper. Sprinkle a few drops of water into the skillet, being sure to let the water hit the bottom of the pan and not the eggs, and immediately cover the skillet with a lid. Let the eggs cook until the whites are cooked through but the yolks are still a bit wobbly, just a minute or two. And that is that.

Warm Grilled Eggplant + Tomato Salad with Herbs

SERVES 4

I spend all winter dreaming about summer produce, which I always try to remember when I'm faced with a bunch of tomatoes and eggplants and I'm wondering what to do with them. After lots of plain tomato salads and boring grilled eggplant, you sometimes need a little something more. This warm salad is just the thing. A slightly spicy mixture of fish sauce, rice vinegar, and jalapeño chile dresses the vegetables, and herbs are used in generous portions. It's one of the things I love the most about Vietnamese cooking: herbs are more than a garnish; they're the anchor. If you don't have an outdoor grill, roast the eggplant as instructed for the Stir-Fried Roasted Eggplant with Pork (page 133) and proceed as directed with the rest of the recipe. You can make the salad ahead, too, and serve it at room temperature.

2 Tbsp fish sauce

2 Tbsp rice vinegar

1 shallot, minced

½ jalapeño chile, seeds discarded and minced

½ cup [120 ml] olive oil

Kosher salt

2 lb [910 g] eggplant (about 2 medium), ends trimmed and cut into slices ¾ in [2 cm] thick

3 large ripe tomatoes, cored and cut into medium wedges

A small handful of fresh mint leaves (a little bit of stem is fine!), torn in half if large

A small handful of fresh basil leaves (a little bit of stem is fine!), torn in half if large

A small handful of fresh cilantro leaves (a little bit of stem is fine!)

In a large bowl, whisk together the fish sauce, vinegar, shallot, jalapeño, and ¼ cup [60 ml] of the olive oil. Season the dressing to taste with salt and reserve it.

Get your outdoor grill going (gas or charcoal) with high heat and make sure the grate is superclean.

Brush the eggplant slices on both sides with the remaining ¼ cup [60 ml] olive oil and sprinkle liberally with salt. Grill the eggplant, turning the slices a few times as they cook, until softened and lightly charred all over, about 10 minutes all together. Transfer the eggplant to a cutting board and roughly chop it.

Add the eggplant to the bowl of dressing along with the tomatoes and all of the herbs. Gently mix everything together. Transfer to a serving platter or bowl and serve immediately while the eggplant is still warm.

Vietnamese Iced Coffee

SERVES 4

When I got to spend a little time in Austin working with Tom and Larry on their book, I became a bit addicted to drinking this coffee in the morning at the bar at Elizabeth Street Café. If you need to get a lot of writing done for a cookbook or any other work, this caffeinated, sugary beverage is basically rocket fuel.

Crushed ice for serving

7 oz [200 g] sweetened condensed milk (one-half of a standard can), or more to taste

4 cups [960 ml] hot strong brewed chicory-flavored coffee (preferably Café Du Monde brand)

Fill four glasses with ice and divide the sweetened condensed milk and coffee among them. Stir each well to combine (or just combine everything in a pitcher, stir, and then divide among the glasses). Serve immediately.

It's Me Again

STEAK + KIMCHI QUESADILLAS

Thinly slice any leftover steak and finely chop about half as much drained cabbage kimchi as you have steak. Sprinkle flour tortillas with a thin layer of Cheddar cheese and divide the steak and kimchi evenly among them. Fold the tortillas into half-moons and cook them on a lightly oiled griddle (or a nonstick skillet) until both sides are lightly browned and the cheese is melted, about 3 minutes per side. Alternatively, heat two sheet pans in a 425°F [220°C] oven, spray one pan with baking spray, place the quesadillas on the sprayed pan, spray the tops of the quesadillas with baking spray, and then put the second sheet pan on top. Bake the quesadillas, sandwiched between the sheet pans, until both sides are golden brown and the cheese is melted, about 10 minutes. This is an easy way to do a lot at once.

EGGPLANT DIP

Pull the tomato wedges out of the eggplant salad and hold onto them. Put the dressed eggplant with all of the herbs and everything else into a food processer and pulse until it has gone from salad to dip, making it as rustic or as smooth as you like. Season it to taste with salt and pepper and transfer it to a serving bowl. Finely chop the leftover dressed tomatoes and pile them on top of the dip. Really delicious served with cucumber slices, rice crackers, and/or shrimp chips.

VIETNAMESE ICED COFFEE GRANITA

Pour whatever Vietnamese Iced Coffee you have left (minus the ice cubes) in a baking dish and place in the freezer. Scrape the mixture every 30 minutes or so until it is flaky and frozen, about 2½ hours total. Scoop into shallow bowls or small glasses for serving. Top with unsweetened whipped cream to enjoy the satisfying mixture of crunchy with creamy and smooth.

COFFEE + BRIOCHE FRENCH TOAST

Pour whatever Vietnamese Iced Coffee you have left (minus the ice cubes) in a shallow bowl or baking dish. For every 1 cup [240 ml], add an egg and whisk well to combine. Soak thick slices of brioche in the mixture (both sides) and cook in a generously buttered nonstick skillet until crisp on both sides. Serve drizzled with extra sweetened condensed milk.

Simple Backpack
Picnic Lunch

PRESSED BROCCOLI RABE + MOZZARELLA SANDWICHES

NECTARINES + PEANUTS IN THEIR SHELLS

HIKERS' COOKIES

The only reason I ever get genuinely excited about hiking is the promise of a well-deserved sandwich with a view. This menu is exactly what I once packed for Grace and me when we took our dogs on a memorable hike near our home. And by memorable, I mean to say mostly terrible. I had inadvertently suggested a route that was almost impossible to find, and once we finally reached the beginning, we quickly realized we would be going up a steep incline of slippery gravel on a day that seemed ten times hotter and more humid that the forecast said it would be. Grace, needless to say, wasn't too excited about the situation I had put us in, and we spent most of the first half of the hike with our heads down and just trying to keep our dogs on the path. When we reached the peak, the promised waterfall turned out to be undeniably beautiful and we untied our shoes and put our feet into the water. I unpacked lunch and gave Grace a sandwich, and we had a good laugh. The power of a good sandwich! The way down was a lot more fun, and there even seemed to be a breeze.

UP TO 1 MONTH AHEAD	Make the cookie dough, portion it, place on a parchment paper–lined sheet pan, and put the whole thing into the freezer. Once the dough is frozen, pop the pieces into an airtight freezer bag. Bake the cookies directly from the freezer.
UP TO 1 DAY AHEAD	Bake the cookies, let cool, and store in a tightly covered container at room temperature. Cook the broccoli rabe and make the olive mixture for the sandwiches. Store in separate covered containers in the refrigerator.
UP TO A FEW HOURS AHEAD	Assemble the sandwiches, wrap them up, and press them.
LAST MOMENT	Pack your picnic and hit the trail!

Pressed Broccoli Rabe + Mozzarella Sandwiches

SERVES 4

I love these sandwiches. They're a vegetarian cross between a New Orleans–style muf-fuletta (hey olive salad!) and a Philadelphia-style pork and broccoli rabe sandwich. They're also inspired by a passage I once read about how legendary food writer M. F. K. Fisher made a guest sit on a wrapped sandwich while they chatted so it would be perfectly pressed in time for lunch. Ha! When these sandwiches are pressed, the olive and caper mixture soaks into the bread and the cheese and garlicky broccoli rabe become really good friends. The broccoli rabe can also be served as a side dish with the olive mixture spooned on top (or you can mix the lot with cooked pasta and call it dinner). If you can't find or don't like broccoli rabe, substitute regular broccoli or any dark, leafy green such as kale.

Kosher salt

¾ lb [340 g] broccoli rabe (an average bunch), tough stems discarded, roughly chopped

3 Tbsp olive oil

2 large garlic cloves, minced

Pinch of red pepper flakes

¼ cup [40 g] green olives, pitted and finely chopped

1½ Tbsp drained brined capers, finely chopped

1 Tbsp red wine vinegar

4 individual-size sandwich rolls, split (I like rolls with sesame seeds for this, but you do you)

1 lb [455 g] fresh mozzarella cheese, sliced

Pour water to a depth of 1 in [2.5 cm] into a medium pot and set over high heat. When the water boils, add a large pinch of salt and then the broccoli rabe and cook, stirring, until bright green and slightly wilted, about 30 seconds. Drain the broccoli rabe in a colander, wipe the pot dry, and return it to high heat. Add 2 Tbsp of the olive oil, the garlic, and the red pepper flakes and stir the garlic into the oil until it's fragrant, just 15 seconds. Immediately add the drained broccoli rabe and a large pinch of salt and cook, stirring, until the broccoli rabe is coated with the garlicky oil and is a bit more softened, about 3 minutes. Remove from the heat and set the broccoli rabe aside to cool down a bit.

In a small bowl, combine the olives, capers, vinegar, the remaining 1 Tbsp olive oil, and a small pinch of salt and stir together. Place the rolls, cut-side up, on a work surface and evenly distribute the olive mixture among the rolls, putting some on both halves of each roll. Divide the mozzarella and broccoli rabe evenly among the rolls, close the rolls, and then tightly wrap each sandwich in plastic wrap. Place something flat and heavy on top of the sand-wiches, such as a large cast-iron skillet. Let the sandwiches sit under this weight for at least an hour before eating or putting them in your backpack.

Nectarines + Peanuts in Their Shells

This is not a recipe. It's just a suggestion to pack nectarines or other similar fruit, like plums or peaches, in a container, paper bag, or plastic bag that's filled with peanuts in their shells. The peanuts will act as literal packing peanuts and will keep the fruit from getting bruised in your backpack, plus you get an extra snack out of the arrangement. I take no credit for this idea: it's all Lee Bailey, the late, great cookbook author.

Hikers' Cookies

MAKES 12 COOKIES

These are kinda, sorta healthy since they're made with whole wheat flour and oats, plus a good dose of ground flaxseed. They're also not too sweet, and the sweet itself comes from maple syrup and not plain old sugar. If all of that sounds as good as a piece of cardboard, know that there's also plenty of butter and add-ins such as dark chocolate and coconut. I love making these for a hike in place of a granola bar because they offer very similar satisfaction and long-lasting energy and they are a cookie and not a granola bar, and cookies > granola bars.

½ cup [110 g] unsalted butter, at room temperature

¼ cup [80 g] maple syrup

2 eggs

2 tsp vanilla extract

½ tsp kosher salt

¾ tsp baking soda

1½ tsp ground cinnamon

1 cup [100 g] old-fashioned rolled oats

½ cup [70 g] whole wheat flour

3 Tbsp ground flaxseed

¾ cup [about 100 g] add-ins such as dark chocolate chips, unsweetened dried fruit, unsweetened flaked dried coconut, and/or chopped nuts

Preheat your oven to 350°F [180°C]. Line a sheet pan with parchment paper.

In a large bowl, combine the butter, maple syrup, eggs, vanilla, salt, baking soda, and cinnamon. Use a handheld electric mixer on medium speed or a whisk to mix everything together well (don't fret if it's not totally smooth and evenly colored; the butter will look like small flakes of rice suspended in a cinnamony batter). Use a wooden spoon to fold in the oats, flour, ground flaxseed, and add-ins.

Use two soupspoons to divide the dough into twelve equal balls (each ball will be about 2 Tbsp dough) and space them evenly on the prepared sheet pan.

Bake the cookies until dark brown, puffed up, and wonderfully fragrant, about 15 minutes. Let the cookies cool on the pan on a wire rack for at least 10 minutes before transferring them to the rack to cool completely. They will crisp a bit as they cool. Leftovers can be stored in an airtight container at room temperature for up to 3 days.

It's Me Again

BROCCOLI RABE PESTO

Put leftover cooked broccoli rabe (and any of the olive mixture from the sandwiches, if you like) into a food processor. For every handful of broccoli rabe, add a small handful of lightly toasted nuts (pine nuts, walnuts, almonds, hazelnuts, or pecans work well) and pulse until finely chopped. Add a small handful of finely grated Parmesan or pecorino cheese and pulse to combine, then add just enough olive oil to turn the mixture into a paste (about 2 Tbsp). Season to taste with salt. Feel free to add some grated lemon zest, too. Delicious on eggs or pasta.

BROCCOLI RABE + FARRO SALAD

For every serving of cooked broccoli rabe (and its olive mixture), prepare a serving of farro (a chewy, nutty grain that's one of wheat's ancient cousins). I simmer it in salted water until softened, about 30 minutes, and then drain it (like pasta). You could use any whole grain instead of farro. Mix the warm farro and broccoli rabe together and add a healthy pour of olive oil, a squeeze of lemon or a splash of vinegar, and salt to taste. Serve at room temperature. Crumbled feta is really good on top.

EASY NECTARINE CRUMBLE

Any leftover nectarines and Hikers' Cookies can be turned into a wonderful crumble. Pit the nectarines, cut them into wedges, and place the wedges in a baking dish (I don't bother peeling them, but feel free if you'd like). Season to taste with granulated or brown sugar and fresh lemon juice (the amounts will depend on how sweet your nectarines are). Add a shake of flour and toss to combine (this will help thicken the juices). Crumble the cookies on top to form a thin, even layer and dot with a little bit of unsalted butter. If you're out of cookies (hey, it happens), mix equal parts old-fashioned rolled oats, all-purpose flour or whole wheat flour, light brown sugar, and unsalted butter together and crumble the mixture on top of the fruit. Bake the crumble at 400°F [200°C] until the top is golden brown and the nectarine juices are bubbling, about 30 minutes. Serve warm with vanilla ice cream.

Afternoon Tacos

SUPER CRUNCHY LIME-Y SALAD

KALE + MUSHROOM TACO FILLING

CHORIZO + POTATO TACO FILLING

WARM CORN TORTILLAS + LETTUCE LEAVES

LIME + HOT SAUCE CREMA

CHARRED TOMATILLO + SCALLION SALSA

PINEAPPLE MARGARITAS

My friend JJ Goode is a fellow cookbook writer and is also one of the funniest people I know. He has collaborated with some of the greatest folks and I particularly love the books that JJ has worked on with Roberto Santibañez (*Truly Mexican* and *Tacos, Tortas, and Tamales*). Not long after JJ and Katie, his very smart and awesome wife, welcomed their son, Remy, into the world, Grace and I stopped by their place for a visit. While we were admiring Remy's laughter, JJ put a Roberto-inspired meal together. There was a skillet of chorizo and potatoes alongside a stack of warm tortillas and a *molcajete* (a stone mortar) filled with tomatillo salsa. There was a simple salad and some ice cream for dessert. It was all very easy and incredibly good.

JJ and I talk often about the really fun, albeit unusual, work we both do collaborating on other people's books. We compare notes about the recipes, ingredients, and skills we've learned from these collaborations and have woven into our own lives. From Roberto's kitchen to JJ's to mine, this inspired menu is all about having a few friends over for a relaxed, welcoming meal.

UP TO 3 DAYS AHEAD	Make the salsa and the *crema* and store in covered containers in the refrigerator.
	Shred the vegetables for the salad, wrap in ever-so-damp paper towels, and store in a plastic bag or an airtight container in the refrigerator. Wash the kale for the taco filling and store the same way.
UP TO 1 DAY AHEAD	Mix the pitcher of margaritas (don't combine with ice just yet) and refrigerate.
UP TO A FEW HOURS AHEAD	Make and dress the salad. Make both of the taco fillings and leave them in their skillets (warm them over low heat just before serving).
	Take the salsa out of the refrigerator and let it come to room temperature. Season it to taste with more lime juice and salt if needed.
LAST MOMENT	Pour the margaritas over ice.
	Warm the tortillas; put out the salad, both of the fillings, the warm tortillas, and all of the toppings.

Super Crunchy Lime-y Salad

SERVES 4

I make a version of this salad, which borders on slaw, nearly every day. Any crunchy vegetables can be added, like thinly sliced radishes or celery or even shaved fennel or kohlrabi. It's the perfect way to use up lots of the bits and bobs kicking around in the refrigerator. I often put a big pile of the salad on my dinner plate and end up not only eating it alongside my tacos but also spooning some of it on top of the tacos (which I highly recommend).

2 Tbsp fresh lime juice

2 Tbsp olive oil

1 small garlic clove, minced

1 tsp red chile paste (like sambal oelek) or hot sauce

½ tsp kosher salt, plus more as needed

1 large heart romaine lettuce, thinly sliced

½ lb [230 g] red cabbage (about ¼ small head), cored and thinly sliced

2 carrots, peeled and coarsely grated

A large handful of fresh cilantro leaves (a little bit of stem is fine!), roughly chopped

¼ cup [35 g] pumpkin seeds, lightly toasted

In a large bowl, whisk together the lime juice, olive oil, garlic, chile paste, and salt. Add the romaine, cabbage, carrots, cilantro, and pumpkin seeds and stir well to combine. Taste and adjust the seasoning with salt and serve.

Kale + Mushroom Taco Filling

SERVES 4

Combining meaty mushrooms and hearty kale makes this vegan filling totally satisfying. It also doubles as a great side dish. You can substitute any dark, leafy green for the kale. I especially like it made with spicy mustard greens.

1 lb [455 g] wild and/or cremini mushrooms

3 Tbsp olive oil

1 tsp cumin seeds, or ½ tsp ground cumin

Kosher salt

2 garlic cloves, minced

1 bunch Lacinato kale, about ½ lb [230 g], tough stems discarded, thinly sliced (or curly kale, roughly chopped)

Pop the tough stems off of the mushrooms by hand and discard them or save them for another use such as vegetable stock (you can even stash these stems along with other vegetable trimmings in an airtight bag in the freezer, wait until the bag is full, and then make stock). Roughly chop the mushrooms and keep them close.

In a large, heavy skillet over high heat, warm the olive oil. Add the cumin seeds and once they begin to sizzle, which should happen just about immediately, add the mushrooms and sprinkle with a large pinch of salt. Turn down the heat to medium and cook, stirring now and then, until the mushrooms have released their liquid and have softened and browned a bit, about 10 minutes.

Turn the heat back up to high, add the garlic and kale, and sprinkle with another large pinch of salt. Stir to combine and then cover the skillet (if your kale is wet from washing, don't even worry about the lid, as the dampness will create steam, which is very welcome). Cook until the kale is bright green and just tender, about 1½ minutes. Serve warm.

Chorizo + Potato Taco Filling

SERVES 4

This taco filling has all of the familiar and gratifying appeal of really good corned beef hash. Boiling the potatoes before crisping them in the skillet might seem like an annoying step that dirties an extra pot, but it's the best way to make sure they're tender. If you can't find fresh chorizo, substitute finely chopped cured chorizo or use ground pork plus a couple of minced garlic cloves and a spoonful each cayenne pepper and sweet or smoked paprika.

1½ lb [680 g] baking potatoes (about 2 large), scrubbed and cut into ½-in [12-mm] cubes

Kosher salt

2 Tbsp canola or other neutral oil, plus more as needed

¾ lb [340 g] fresh chorizo, casings discarded

1 small red onion, finely diced

A large handful of fresh cilantro leaves (a little bit of stem is fine!), finely chopped

In a large saucepan, combine the potatoes, water to cover by about 1 in [2.5 cm], and 1 Tbsp salt and set over high heat. Bring the water to a boil, lower the heat to medium, and simmer until the potatoes are just tender, about 8 minutes. Drain the potatoes in a colander and give them a really good shake to make sure they're as dry as possible. Let the potatoes hang out while you get the chorizo going.

Put the oil into a large nonstick skillet over high heat and crumble the chorizo into it. Cook, stirring now and then, until the chorizo has released its liquid, the liquid has evaporated, and the meat begins to sizzle in all of its glorious fat, about 8 minutes.

Add the drained potatoes and the onion and cook, stirring now and then, until everything has nice crispy edges, about 8 more minutes. Between the nonstick skillet and the fat from your chorizo, you shouldn't need any more oil for this, but if things are looking dry and your potatoes aren't crisping nicely, go ahead and add another splash of oil. Season the mixture to taste with salt and sprinkle with the cilantro. Serve warm.

Warm Corn Tortillas + Lettuce Leaves

No recipe here, just some thoughts. To warm corn tortillas, I like to char them directly on the flame of my gas stove or outdoor grill, stack them on an ever-so-damp kitchen towel, and then wrap them up so they can steam and soften a bit. This way you get all of the flavor of the char and all of the softness of steam, plus the stacked tortillas stay cozy and warm when they're wrapped up. If you eat corn tortillas often, consider buying an inexpensive tortilla warmer (the thick plastic ones look kind of cheesy but are very effective) for serving to keep them nice and hot. The warmer really works! Or just serve enough tortillas for the first round of tacos and then heat up another batch as you go. Lettuce leaves are pretty self-explanatory and a great option for those who can't eat tortillas for any reason or would just prefer a lighter option.

Lime + Hot Sauce Crema

MAKES 1 CUP [240 ML]

Drizzling this sauce on your tacos adds richness and brightness at the same time and how about that? If you're vegan, substitute Vegenaise or vegan sour cream for the sour cream. Other than the chorizo filling option, the rest of this meal is totally vegan (including margaritas).

¾ cup [180 g] sour cream

2 Tbsp whole milk or water

2 Tbsp fresh lime juice

1 Tbsp of your favorite hot sauce

½ tsp kosher salt

In a medium bowl, whisk together the sour cream, milk, lime juice, hot sauce, and salt and that is that.

Charred Tomatillo + Scallion Salsa

MAKES ABOUT 1½ CUPS [360 ML]

This salsa will cause you never to buy another jar of salsa. It's seriously that good, and almost surprisingly so because it's so easy to make. It's not only vegan but also totally free of all of the things that people tend to point out (fat, sugar, dairy, gluten, and so on). I like this salsa best just after it's made, when the lime juice and cilantro still have their freshness, but it's also totally fine to make it up to 3 days in advance and store it in a covered container in the refrigerator. Keep in mind that cooked and cooled tomatillos tend to gel, almost like really good chicken stock, so don't worry if the salsa seems a little thick when you take it out of the fridge. Be sure to let it come to room temperature before serving and then maybe give it an extra squeeze of lime and a sprinkle of salt to perk it up.

¾ lb [340 g] tomatillos (about 8 small or 6 large), husked and rinsed, roughly chopped

6 scallions, tough roots and dark green tops trimmed off, white and light green parts roughly chopped

1 jalapeño chile, roughly chopped (discard the seeds if you like)

2 garlic cloves, peeled

3 Tbsp fresh lime juice

A large handful of fresh cilantro leaves (a little bit of stem is fine!)

1 tsp kosher salt

Position an oven rack about 6 in [15 cm] from the heat source and preheat your broiler. Line a large sheet pan with aluminum foil.

Place the tomatillos, scallions, jalapeño, and garlic cloves on the prepared sheet pan and broil, taking the pan out to stir the vegetables now and then, until they're charred in spots and softened a bit, about 8 minutes all together, depending on the strength of your broiler.

Transfer all of the broiled vegetables to a blender or food processor, add the lime juice, cilantro, and salt and pulse until puréed but not completely smooth (texture is good!).

Alternatively, put the broiled tomatillos into a medium bowl and crush them with a potato masher. Finely chop the scallions, chile, garlic, and cilantro, add to the mashed tomatillos along with the lime juice and salt, and stir well.

Serve the salsa at room temperature.

Pineapple Margaritas

SERVES 4

These margaritas are the perfect balance of tart lime juice and sweet pineapple juice, plus, of course, the punch of a generous tequila pour. The sparkling water gives them a little fizz and also helps the drink last a bit longer. If you like your margaritas with spicy salted rims, add a little coarse red chile powder to the salt for extra spark (or the home-made tajín from page 187).

½ cup [120 ml] fresh lime juice

1½ cups [360 ml] pineapple juice

1 cup [240 ml] silver tequila

1 cup [240 ml] sparkling water

Kosher salt

1 lime, thinly sliced

Crushed ice for serving

4 small wedges fresh pine-apple (optional)

Put the lime juice, pineapple juice, tequila, and sparkling water into a tall pitcher and stir well to combine.

Make a thin layer of salt on a small plate. Rub a lime slice around the rims of four highball glasses. One at a time, tip the glasses upside-down onto the salt to coat the rims. Fill each glass with ice and evenly divide the pineapple mixture among them. Garnish each drink with a few lime slices and a pineapple wedge (if using). Serve immediately.

It's Me Again

TACO FILLING HASH

Put whatever kale and mushrooms and potatoes and chorizo are left over from your taco fillings into a hot skillet that you've slicked with a bit of olive oil. Cook, stirring, until everything is warmed through. As the mixture heats, use a metal spatula to press down on it to crush the potatoes a bit so they'll sort of bind everything together. Be sure to let the mixture brown and crisp, as that's the best part of hash. Season to taste with salt and serve with eggs (poached, over easy, scrambled—whatever makes you happy).

CHILAQUILES VERDES

Cut any leftover tortillas into strips or triangles and fry in a little hot oil (see page 184 for more instructions on how to do this) until nice and crisp (or use store-bought chips). For every handful of tortilla chips, put about ¼ cup [60 ml] leftover Charred Tomatillo + Scallion Salsa into a large pot, bring to a simmer, add the chips, and cook almost as if the chips are greens (imagine that!) that you are just looking to wilt, about 1 minute. They should be softened but still have a little bite. Transfer the chilaquiles to a serving platter and drizzle with whatever Lime + Hot Sauce Crema you have left and top with whatever Super Crunchy Lime-y Salad you have left (if you don't have any left, just top with some thinly sliced radishes and/or scallions, plus some roughly chopped fresh cilantro).

Fourth of July

FROZEN WATERMELON AGUAS FRESCAS

LAMB BURGERS WITH GRILLED RED ONIONS

GRILLED OKRA + CORN WITH LEMON + RED CHILE

GRANDMA'S CUCUMBER SALAD

WHOLE WHEAT BERRY SHORTCAKES

I spent some of the most memorable summers of my childhood at a sleep-away camp for girls in Maine. The Fourth of July was always a big deal because it was the only national holiday to coincide with our time at camp. We would start the day by participating in the local four-mile road race in the neighboring town (four on the Fourth!), which benefitted the local library, and then there was always a big moment about raising the flag, followed by an all-American cookout with burgers and hot dogs and the works. Being at camp on the Fourth of July provided plenty of tradition and routine, just as holidays typically do wherever you are. It was a patriotic celebration without question. As I've gotten older, I've started to ask more questions, and I've come to more fully appreciate the annual pause to reflect on the idea of independence and all of its nuances.

I've also spent a lot of time thinking about what exactly America is and how our food reflects our country. When it comes to preparing the country's birthday meal, I've embraced the opportunity to combine the old with the new, the established and expected with a few twists that better represent all of the shades that are woven into our fabric. This menu includes many traditional American foods (watermelon, burgers, shortcake), but all with a bit more variety, including some personal family favorites. At the end of the day, what makes American food great is that it reflects and represents all of us. And all of us, our stories included, should have a place at the table.

UP TO 1 DAY AHEAD

Make the cucumber salad and store in a covered container in the refrigerator.

Make the watermelon aguas frescas minus the ice, cover, and store in the refrigerator.

Make the sauce for the burgers and store in a covered container in the refrigerator.

UP TO A FEW HOURS AHEAD

Bake the biscuits for the shortcakes (warm them in a 300°F/150°C oven or toaster oven before serving). Whip the cream for the shortcakes and keep it in a covered bowl in the refrigerator (you might want to give it an extra whisking right before serving). Mix the berries for the shortcakes and store covered at room temperature.

LAST MOMENT

Blend the watermelon agua frescas with the ice, grill the burgers and vegetables, taste and adjust the seasoning of the cucumber salad (sometimes it needs a little extra salt or vinegar before serving).

Assemble the shortcakes.

Frozen Watermelon Aguas Frescas

SERVES 4

When cold water just won't cut it on a hot day, turn to this icy watermelon drink. A kind of mash-up between a Mexican agua fresca and an all-American slushie, it's the definition of refreshing. Be sure to blend together everything except the ice before you add the ice so the honey is fully incorporated into the mixture, rather than frozen in bits and pieces on the ice.

1 lb [455 g] bite-size cubes ripe seedless watermelon (about 3 cups)

2 cups [480 ml] water

½ cup [120 ml] fresh lime juice

2 Tbsp honey or sugar

3 cups [540 g] ice cubes

Combine the watermelon, water, lime juice, and honey in a blender and blend until smooth. Add the ice and blend again until the mixture is smooth. If your blender is not large enough to hold everything at once, combine half of the watermelon mixture with half of the ice and then repeat. Divide the mixture among four glasses and serve immediately.

Lamb Burgers with Grilled Red Onions

SERVES 4

When you want a good old backyard hamburger but also crave something a bit more interesting, swap beef for lamb and get creative with your toppings. The burgers themselves are simple, but the accompanying creamy dill sauce, grilled red onions, and toasted buns amplify them. If you don't have a grill, just cook the onions and burgers in separate hot cast-iron skillets on your stove top with the fan on and the windows open (or you can broil them both).

¼ cup [60 g] mayonnaise

2 Tbsp fresh lemon juice

1 garlic clove, minced

A small handful of fresh dill fronds, finely chopped

Kosher salt

2 large red onions, cut into slices ¾ in [2 cm] thick

2 Tbsp olive oil

1 lb [455 g] ground lamb, at room temperature

4 hamburger buns (preferably Martin's potato rolls or any other soft bun)

4 large leaves butter lettuce (also known as Bibb or Boston lettuce)

4 large tomato slices

In a small bowl, whisk together the mayonnaise, lemon juice, garlic, and dill. Season the mixture to taste with salt and reserve it.

Get your outdoor grill going (gas or charcoal) with high heat and make sure the grate is superclean. If your grill needs it, brush the grate with some neutral oil (I like to fold up a paper towel and drizzle it with oil and then use tongs to rub it on the grate).

Put the onions on a sheet pan (or whatever you will use to carry them to the grill) and drizzle with the olive oil and season liberally with salt. Use your hands to make sure the onions are well coated. You can stick a metal skewer (or a wooden skewer that's been soaked in water for at least 15 minutes) horizontally through each onion slice to keep it together while it grills (I can never be bothered to do this, but it does work well if you get stressed about flipping things on the grill).

Divide the lamb into four equal portions and shape each portion into a thin patty. Aggressively sprinkle both sides of each patty with salt (don't be shy).

Place the onions and the patties on the grill and cook them, turning them as little as possible, until the burgers are nicely browned on both sides and firm to the touch, about 3 minutes per side, and the onions are browned and softened, about 5 minutes per side. Transfer the burgers and onions to a sheet pan or something else large to collect them as they're done and let them hang out while you toast the buns. Place the buns, cut-side down, on the grill until lightly toasted, about 30 seconds.

Arrange the buns, cut-side up, on a work surface. Divide the mayonnaise mixture evenly among the toasted sides and spread to cover. Place a burger on the bottom half of each bun and divide the onions, tomatoes, and lettuce among them. Put the tops on the burgers and serve *immediately*.

Grilled Okra + Corn with Lemon + Red Chile

SERVES 4

There are a lot of things, including politics and cilantro, that seem to divide the world in two, and okra is definitely one of them. Folks seem to love it or hate it. I often think the divide comes from poor experiences, and as a proud lover of okra, I highly suggest grilling it to create converts. Instead of slipping away into a slimy braise or disappearing under breading in a deep fryer, grilled okra stays firm and juicy and is one of the best ways to enjoy it, not to mention one of the easiest ways to prepare it. Here, I combine okra with corn for a mixed grill that's both colorful and delicious, especially when topped with bright lemon and spicy chile. If your grill grate has particularly wide bars, you can put a sheet of aluminum foil, a large griddle, or a mesh grill topper on the grate so you don't lose anything through the bars. If you don't have an outdoor grill, try straddling a grill pan over two stove-top burners or just blast the corn and okra in a very hot oven (like 450°F/230°C).

1 lb [455 g] fresh okra

4 ears corn, shucked, cut into 2-in [5-cm] lengths

½ cup [120 ml] olive oil

Kosher salt

3 Tbsp fresh lemon juice

1 Tbsp honey

1 small fresh red chile, minced, or 1 Tbsp red chile paste (like sambal oelek)

Get your outdoor grill going (gas or charcoal) with high heat and make sure the grate is superclean.

Put the okra and corn on a sheet pan, drizzle with ¼ cup [60 ml] of the olive oil, and sprinkle with 1 tsp kosher salt. Use your hands to make sure all of the vegetables are well coated.

Carefully place the okra and corn on the grill, making sure they don't fall between the bars of the grate (if the bars are particularly wide, check out my suggestions in the headnote). Grill the vegetables, turning them a few times as they cook, until lightly charred all over, about 10 minutes all together. Transfer the vegetables to a serving platter.

Meanwhile, in a small bowl, whisk together the remaining ¼ cup [60 ml] olive oil, lemon juice, honey, chile, and ½ tsp kosher salt. Drizzle over the okra and corn. Serve warm or at room temperature.

Grandma's Cucumber Salad

SERVES 4

Each and every time I make this I am immediately transported to my grandparents' kitchen. My grandma used to make this to go with just about every single meal, and it goes well with just about everything. The sound and even the smell of a fork being run down the side of a peeled cucumber, its tines creating wavy lines, is such a distinct childhood memory for me. You can make this a day ahead of time (or even a couple of days) and just refrigerate it in a closed container. My cousin Jenette swears it only gets better the longer it sits. Be sure to season it once more before serving.

1 Tbsp canola or other neutral oil

1 Tbsp distilled white vinegar or apple cider vinegar

1 tsp sugar

1 tsp kosher salt

1 lb [455 g] cucumbers (about 2 regular), ends trimmed, peeled

1 small white onion, cut into thin half-moons

In a large bowl, whisk together the canola oil, vinegar, sugar, and salt until the sugar and salt dissolve.

Run the tines of a fork lengthwise down the sides of the cucumbers and then thinly slice them crosswise. Add the cucumbers and onion to the bowl with the vinegar mixture and mix well. Then, as my grandmother says, "taste if it needs anything and add it." That means, season to taste with more vinegar, sugar, and/or salt if needed.

Serve immediately or, better yet, cover and refrigerate for a couple of hours (or up to 24 hours) before serving so the cucumbers soften a little. If you do make it ahead, be sure to season it to taste before serving, as it might need a bit more salt and vinegar to shine.

Whole Wheat Berry Shortcakes

SERVES 4

I was fifteen when my paternal grandfather turned seventy-five. As a fledgling entre-preneur, I offered to cater his birthday party for about forty people, held in a tent on my grandparents' lawn. I didn't quite realize what I had signed myself up for, and I remember wiping my brow while I furiously grilled dozens of skewers of tuna satay on my George Foreman Grill (ha!) to go with some sort of wasabi dip. The rest of the menu was equally questionable and I don't remember much, but I sure do remember dessert. My grandfather adored blueberries more than just about anything, so instead of a cake, I made individual biscuits and plated blueberry shortcakes for everyone. This dessert is an homage to that one but updated just a bit. The biscuits are made with all whole wheat flour for some added dimension and also to make them a little healthier. Don't skip the ground ginger in the biscuits—it's seriously good. And instead of just blueberries and whipped cream, I like a mix of them plus strawberries and raspberries to make the whole thing red, white, and blue and for added flavor. If my grandpa was still around, I'd make sure he got all of the blueberries.

1 cup [140 g] whole wheat flour

1½ tsp baking powder

1½ tsp ground ginger

4 Tbsp granulated sugar [50 g] or coconut sugar [35 g], plus a little more for topping biscuits (optional)

½ tsp kosher salt, plus a tiny pinch

2 Tbsp cold unsalted butter, cubed

½ cup [120 ml] buttermilk

2 cups [260 g] mixed berries, hulled if needed and cut into small pieces if large

½ cup [120 ml] heavy cream

1 tsp vanilla extract

Preheat your oven to 450°F [230°C]. Line a sheet pan with parchment paper.

In a large bowl, whisk together the flour, baking powder, ginger, 2 Tbsp of the sugar, and ½ tsp of the salt. Scatter the butter over the flour mixture and use your hands to work in the butter, rubbing it between your fingers, until the mixture is the consistency of coarse crumbs. Using a wooden spoon, gently stir all but 1 Tbsp of the buttermilk into the flour mixture and mix just until combined—no need to mix too thoroughly here.

Turn the dough out onto a clean work surface and pat it out into a rough 5 in [12 cm] square about ½ in [12 mm] thick. Cut the dough into four equal pieces and transfer them to the prepared sheet pan. Be sure to leave some space around each piece. Brush the tops of the biscuits lightly with the remaining 1 Tbsp buttermilk (you might not even need all of it). If you like, sprinkle each biscuit with a little sugar.

(Continued)

Bake the biscuits until they have risen and are golden brown, about 15 minutes.

While the biscuits are baking, put the berries into a large bowl and sprinkle with 1 Tbsp of the remaining sugar and the remaining pinch of salt. Use a fork (or your hands) to crush about one-third of the berries, then give the mixture a good stir. It should be slightly saucy.

In a stand mixer fitted with the whisk attachment, combine the cream, vanilla, and the remaining 1 Tbsp sugar and beat on medium-high speed until soft peaks form, about 2 minutes (or use a bowl and a whisk and some solid effort).

Slice each warm biscuit in half horizontally and place the bottom halves, cut-sides up, on individual plates. Divide the cream and berries evenly among the bottom halves. Top with the biscuit tops and serve immediately while still warm.

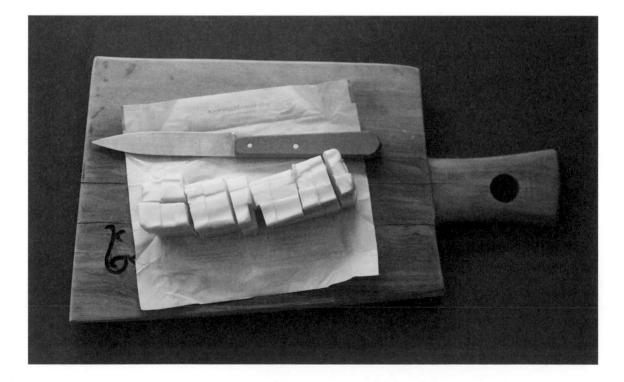

It's Me Again

GRILLED CORN, ONION + OKRA SALAD

Roughly chop any leftover grilled okra and cut the kernels off of any leftover grilled corn. Combine the okra and corn in a large bowl. Roughly chop any leftover grilled red onions from the lamb burgers and add them to the corn and okra. Drizzle the vegetables with just enough olive oil to make them shine and season to taste with red wine vinegar or sherry vinegar, salt, and pepper. Add a handful or two of finely chopped fresh soft herbs (parsley, chives, dill, and/or cilantro all work well in this). Great served at room temperature as part of a larger spread of salads or alongside grilled chicken or fish.

CHILLED CUCUMBER + YOGURT SOUP

Leftover cucumber salad is cold soup waiting to happen. Put it into a blender with whatever juice has accumulated in the bowl along with a large scoop of plain yogurt and purée until smooth. You're looking for a gazpacho-like consistency, so add a bit more yogurt and/or a splash of water as needed. Season the soup to taste with lemon juice, salt, and pepper. I like this soup to have a bit of body, but if you prefer it supersmooth, pass it through a fine-mesh sieve. Serve the soup cold (which it probably already will be if you've taken the cucumber salad and yogurt out of the fridge). It's great with something kind of crunchy on top to provide some textural contrast. This could be croutons, finely diced cucumber, halved cherry or Sungold tomatoes, crumbled feta cheese, or finely chopped toasted almonds. You can also put some cooked shrimp, crab, or even lobster into the bowl before you pour the soup on top for a more substantial and slightly fancy moment.

BURGER BUN SUMMER PUDDING

Use any leftover berry mixture from the shortcakes or get yourself about 3 or 4 cups [390 to 520 g] berries and place in a small saucepan with ¼ cup [50 g] granulated sugar and 2 Tbsp water. Simmer for a minute and then stir in 1 Tbsp fresh lemon juice (or rum!). Ladle one quarter of the mixture into a medium mixing bowl and cover with an even layer of burger bun halves, then repeat twice and top with the final quarter of the berry mixture (so you'll have three layers of buns). Cover with plastic and nestle a plate on top to weigh the whole thing down. Refrigerate for at least 12 hours (and up to 24) before inverting on a platter, slicing, and serving with softly whipped cream. A revelation!

Middle Eastern Dinner Outside

CUCUMBERS WITH SUMAC + WARM PITA

SLICED FETA + CHERRY TOMATO SALAD

GREEK YOGURT WITH FRIED PISTACHIOS + LEMON

GRILLED BEEF + ZUCCHINI MEATBALLS WITH TAHINI DRESSING

YOGURT CAKE WITH FIG PRESERVES

I may have saved the best for last. While I love all of the menus in this book, this one may very well be my favorite. It's the perfect balance of dishes and each one is remarkably easy to prepare. The meatballs are the stars here. Reminiscent of grilled Turkish *köfte*, I started making a version of them one summer when things like burgers and grilled zucchini got boring quickly. By grating the zucchini and combining it with the ground meat and lots of great spices, I ended up with a new obsession. The menu is rounded out with simple side dishes, including some that require no cooking, like a platter of sliced cucumbers and a pile of warm pita bread.

When I was testing these recipes, my card night friends (see page 41) were visiting us, and we all cooked together and bounced around the kitchen with music playing and with Lizzy's baby, Lucy, laughing. It was just perfect. When we sat down to eat, Amelia put our collective feelings into words: "I don't want this meal to start," she said, "because I don't want it to end." Really great friends and simple, wonderful food are the best way to simultaneously press pause and play on life.

UP TO 3 DAYS AHEAD	Make the meatball mixture (don't cook the meatballs yet) and the tahini mixture and store covered in the refrigerator.
UP TO 1 DAY AHEAD	Slice the cucumbers, wrap in ever-so-damp paper towels, and store in a plastic bag or an airtight container in the refrigerator. Make and bake the cake, wrap tightly in plastic wrap, and store at room temperature.
UP TO A FEW HOURS AHEAD	Make the tomato salad, cover, and leave at room temperature. Take the tahini mixture out of the refrigerator so it can come to room temperature.
UP TO 1 HOUR AHEAD	Mix up the yogurt and top with the pistachios.
LAST MOMENT	Grill the meatballs. Warm the pitas, sprinkle the cucumbers with sumac, put out the tomato salad and yogurt, and drizzle the meatballs with the tahini mixture. Slice and serve the cake.

Cucumbers with Sumac
+ Warm Pita

No recipes for these, but here are a few notes. A big platter of sliced cucumbers is sometimes all you need to round out a meal. They give you the freshness and crunch of a salad without any of the hassle of washing and drying greens, plus they're just so refreshing. I like using slim cucumbers here and slicing them on the diagonal, but you do you. If you have some ground sumac, sprinkle it on top. It's beautiful and also quite tart. If you don't have sumac, don't sweat it. Just drizzle the cucumbers with some fresh lemon juice or a splash of vinegar and sprinkle with some salt and coarsely ground red chile powder.

As for the warm pita, buy a package of the best pita breads you can find and then warm them up before you serve them. For this particular meal, I throw them on the grill after I pull the meatballs off and lightly char them on both sides, and then I wrap them in an ever-so-damp kitchen towel (just like corn tortillas) to keep them warm in their cozy huddle. You can instead warm them in a 300°F [150°C] oven and then wrap them in the towel or just microwave them in the towel.

Sliced Feta + Cherry Tomato Salad

SERVES 6

Great summer tomatoes are a cook's best friend because they require so little effort to be good. You basically just need to season them and then get out of their way. It's nice to use a mix of colors and sizes here (I like the small, yellow Sungolds, but use whatever tastes best near where you live). Crushing some of them makes a quick and incredibly easy sauce for the rest.

1 garlic clove, minced

2 Tbsp red wine vinegar, plus more as needed

¼ cup [60 ml] olive oil

1 tsp kosher salt, plus more as needed

1 tsp dried oregano

4 cups [640 g] cherry tomatoes

A small handful of fresh Italian parsley leaves (a little bit of stem is fine!), roughly chopped

A small handful of fresh mint leaves (a little bit of stem is fine!), roughly chopped

½-lb [230-g] block feta cheese, thinly sliced

Put the garlic, vinegar, oil, and salt into a large bowl. Rub the oregano between your fingers as you drop it into the bowl. Whisk everything well to combine. Add one-fourth of the tomatoes and crush them with your hands or a potato masher to release most of their juice. Add the remaining tomatoes and the parsley and mint and stir to mix well. Season the tomatoes to taste with more salt or vinegar if needed (this will depend on the ripeness of your tomatoes).

Arrange half of the feta in a single layer on a serving platter. Place half of the tomato salad on top and then repeat the layers. Serve within a few hours.

Greek Yogurt with Fried Pistachios + Lemon

SERVES 6

This is the easiest thing ever but so good and so memorable. It's wonderful spooned on warm pita and is a really nice treat for your meatballs, sliced cucumbers, and tomato salad to bump into on your plate. This works fine with low-fat or nonfat yogurt, but it's *really* best with full-fat yogurt. Also, if you can't find unsalted pistachios, omit sprinkling them with salt.

¼ cup [60 ml] olive oil

½ cup [70 g] shelled and unsalted pistachio nuts (or walnut halves, pine nuts, or roughly chopped almonds)

¾ tsp kosher salt

3 cups [720 g] plain full-fat Greek yogurt

Finely grated zest and juice of 2 lemons

In a small skillet over medium heat, warm the olive oil. Add the pistachios and cook, stirring, until the pistachios sizzle and turn a slightly darker shade of greenish brown and begin to smell fragrant, about 1 minute. Keep your eye on these as they can go quickly from browned to burned. Turn off the heat and sprinkle the pistachios with ¼ tsp of the salt. Let the pistachios cool to room temperature.

Meanwhile, in a large bowl, whisk together the yogurt, lemon zest and juice, and the remaining ½ tsp salt. Transfer the mixture to a wide serving bowl and use a spoon to spread it in an even layer. Place the pistachios and all of their glorious oil on top of the yogurt. Serve immediately, or cover and leave at room temperature for up to 1 hour before serving.

Grilled Beef + Zucchini Meatballs with Tahini Dressing

SERVES 6

I make these often for Grace because they've got no bread crumbs or other carb binders, which is great if you have type 1 diabetes like she does. That means they are also gluten free, if that's important to you. Plus, they're not boring, which is great no matter what you eat. If you don't have a grill, you can broil the meatballs (using roughly the same timing) or you can roast them on a parchment paper–lined sheet pan in a 425°F [220°C] oven until they're firm to the touch, 20 to 25 minutes. If you weren't serving these with a tomato salad, you could absolutely finish them in a tomato sauce (like the one on page 33 minus the ground turkey). Throw an extra pinch of ground cumin and a cinnamon stick into the sauce.

2 zucchini, ends trimmed and coarsely grated

5 garlic cloves, minced

1 small red onion, coarsely grated or finely chopped

1 egg, lightly beaten

1 Tbsp ground cumin

1 Tbsp nigella seeds (optional)

2 tsp ground coriander

Kosher salt

2 lb [910 g] ground beef

3 Tbsp tahini

3 Tbsp fresh lemon juice

½ cup [120 ml] boiling water, or as needed

A small handful of chopped fresh soft herbs (cilantro, parsley, dill, and/or chives all work well)

Get your outdoor grill going (gas or charcoal) with high heat and make sure the grate is superclean.

Place the grated zucchini in the center of a kitchen towel and gather the towel around it to form a tight bundle. Wring out the zucchini over the sink, really squeezing it as tightly as you can to release all of its excess water. Transfer the zucchini to a large bowl and add the garlic, onion, egg, cumin, nigella seeds (if using), coriander, and 1 Tbsp salt. Mix everything together well, then add the beef and mix until well combined (your hands are the best tools for this job). Form the mixture into golf ball–size meatballs (it will make about 30 meatballs; feel free to make them whatever size you want, really, keeping in mind they will shrink a little as they cook). The mixture will be sticky, so wet your hands with a bit of water to help prevent the meat from sticking to them. Transfer the meatballs to a sheet pan or something else that will hold them in a single layer and then carry them out to your grill.

If your grill needs it, brush the grate with some neutral oil (I like to fold up a paper towel and drizzle it with oil and then use tongs to rub it on the grate). If your grill grate has particularly wide bars, you can put a wire baking rack, a mesh grill topper, or a sheet of aluminum foil on the grate so you don't lose any meatballs through the bars.

(Continued)

Grill the meatballs, turning them a few times as they cook, until browned all over and just firm to the touch, about 10 minutes all together.

Meanwhile, in a small bowl, whisk together the tahini, lemon juice, and boiling water. The mixture should run off of your spoon. If it doesn't, add a splash more boiling water (the amount you need will depend on how thick your tahini is). Season the mixture to taste with salt.

When the meatballs are ready, transfer them to a serving platter and drizzle them with the tahini mixture. Sprinkle with the herbs and serve immediately.

Yogurt Cake with Fig Preserves

SERVES 8

This cake is so wonderfully easy to prepare (one bowl, one pan). The fig preserves give it a wonderful glazed surface, plus you get pieces of fig in the cake. Any flavor of preserves or jam can be used here (apricot is really nice). The cake itself has a dense, almost cheesecake-like, texture that's especially satisfying. It is nice served with extra Greek yogurt spooned on top. I also love this cake for breakfast (hey, it's got yogurt).

2 eggs

1½ cups [360 g] plain full-fat Greek yogurt

4 Tbsp [55 g] unsalted butter, melted and cooled

½ cup [100 g] sugar

2 tsp vanilla extract

2 tsp baking powder

1 tsp baking soda

1 tsp kosher salt

1½ cups [180 g] all-purpose flour

½ cup [150 g] fig preserves

Preheat your oven to 350°F [180°C]. Spray the bottom and sides of an 8-in [20-cm] round cake pan with baking spray and line the bottom with a circle of parchment paper. Spray the parchment paper for good measure and set the pan aside.

In a large bowl, whisk together the eggs, yogurt, butter, sugar, and vanilla, mixing well. Sprinkle the baking powder, baking soda, and salt over the egg mixture and whisk until thoroughly incorporated. Gently stir in the flour until just combined. Use a rubber spatula to scrape the batter into the prepared pan and then smooth the surface so it is even.

Dollop the preserves evenly over the cake batter. Use a small spoon or the tip of a paring knife to swirl the preserves into the batter a bit. The goal is for the cake to have bites of preserves, not to have a preserves-flavored cake (in other words, don't stir them in completely, just swirl them).

Bake the cake until golden brown, firm to the touch, and a toothpick inserted in the center comes out clean (be mindful that it might pick up some preserves), about 55 minutes. Let the cake cool in the pan on a wire rack to room temperature.

Cut into wedges and serve. Leftovers can be wrapped in plastic and stored at room temperature for up to 3 days.

It's Me Again

FATTOUSH

Combine any leftover sliced cucumbers sprinkled with sumac and any leftover tomato salad in a bowl. For every large serving of salad, tear a pita bread into bite-size pieces and toast in a toaster oven or on a sheet pan under the broiler until crisp. Toss the pieces into the salad as if they were croutons and mix well. Add quite a lot of roughly chopped fresh Italian parsley leaves (think of the parsley as more of a salad green than a garnish). If the salad needs a little bit more juice and love (it will of course depend on whatever you started with), drizzle it with olive oil and red wine vinegar and season it to taste with salt and pepper.

TURKISH BREAKFAST

This is just about assembling what you already have in order to create a breakfast spread that's common in Turkey and should be more common everywhere because it's delightful. Put the leftovers from the meal into separate bowls along with bowls of jams or other preserves and olives. It's also nice to have some Turkish cheeses or any soft, fresh cheeses like ricotta and/or a young Manchego. A bowl of grapes is a good addition, too. The idea is to mix and match little bites of the various foods: bread with some cheese and jam, a few cucumbers dipped in yogurt, and so on. Make a pot of strong Turkish coffee and ask a friend to pick up some Turkish pastries on his or her way to your house.

MEATBALL PITA SANDWICHES

Slather pita breads with leftover yogurt and then pile them with leftover meatballs (cold or warmed up . . . both have their appeal) and whatever tahini mixture remains and top with leftover sliced cucumbers, tomatoes, and feta. These are also delicious topped with shredded red cabbage that you've scrunched with salt and vinegar. Tuck a few chopped olives or pickles in there, too, if you like those sorts of things (if you don't, I'll take yours!).

POACHED EGGS WITH YOGURT + FETA

Spoon leftover lemony yogurt (pistachios are welcome, too) on a plate and top with a couple of poached eggs. Sprinkle with feta and some soft herbs if you have them and an extra lemon wedge for squeezing over. Serve with warm pita.

Seven Lists

SEVEN THINGS TO DO WITH LEFTOVER WINE

SEVEN THINGS TO DO WITH COOKED RICE

SEVEN THINGS TO DO WITH TYPICAL
TAKEOUT LEFTOVERS

SEVEN THINGS TO DO WITH
LEFTOVER SNACKS

SEVEN THINGS TO DO WITH
NOT-SO-NEW PRODUCE

SEVEN THINGS TO BRING WHEN
YOU'RE INVITED TO DINNER

SEVEN GREAT THINGS TO DELEGATE

Seven Things to Do with Leftover Wine

Sangria Ice Cubes: Mix leftover wine (any color) with equal amounts of fresh orange juice and freeze in ice-cube trays (the orange juice will help lower the alcohol content so the cubes will freeze more solidly). Once frozen, pop the cubes into an airtight freezer bag and keep on hand to cool down your next pitcher of sangria.

Coq au Vin Blanc: Cut up a whole chicken (or buy one already cut up) and season aggressively with salt and pepper. Heat up a slick of olive oil and a knob of butter in a large, heavy pot and brown the chicken pieces on all sides. Add a finely chopped yellow onion, a few minced garlic cloves, and enough white wine to come halfway up the sides of the chicken. Bring to a boil, lower the heat, cover partially, and simmer until the chicken is incredibly tender, about 45 minutes. If you'd like, just before serving, add a splash of cream or whisk in some crème fraîche to make the sauce extra rich. Good as is or with sautéed or roasted mushrooms folded in at the end. Serve with rice or mashed potatoes.

Braised Pork with Red Wine + Cherries: Cut 2 lb [910 g] boneless pork shoulder into bite-size pieces and season aggressively with salt and pepper. Heat up a slick of olive oil in a large, heavy pot and brown the pork well (work in batches as necessary). Add a thinly sliced large red onion, 2 large handfuls of dried cherries, and enough red wine to come halfway up the sides of the pork. Bring to a boil, turn off the heat, and cover. Finish cooking in a 300°F [150°C] oven, stirring now and then, until the pork is very tender, about 2 hours. Ideally, refrigerate the pork overnight and then gently warm it the next day over low heat (it always tastes better the next day). Serve with creamy polenta, egg noodles, or rice—anything to soak up all of the rich sauce.

Drunken Spaghetti: Pour whatever red wine you have left over in a large pot and add enough water to total about 4 qt [3.7 L] liquid. Bring to a boil, add 1 lb [455 g] spaghetti, and cook until just al dente. Scoop out 1 cup [240 ml] of the cooking liquid, then drain the spaghetti, return it to the pot, and add the reserved cooking liquid and 3 Tbsp unsalted butter. Cook over low heat, tossing, until the spaghetti has absorbed a lot of the liquid and the mixture is saucy, about 2 minutes. Add 2 large handfuls of finely grated Parmesan or pecorino cheese and then serve with extra cheese on top.

Red Wine Onions: Thinly slice 2 lb [910 g] red onions (about 4 medium) and cook down in a little bit of olive oil, stirring now and then, until softened, about 15 minutes. Sprinkle with ¼ cup [50 g] packed dark brown sugar and 1 tsp each salt and red pepper flakes. Add 2 cups [480 ml] red wine. Boil, stirring now and then, until most of the liquid evaporates and the onions are collapsed and concentrated, about 30 minutes. Taste and adjust the seasoning with salt and/or brown sugar if needed. Store in a covered container in the refrigerator for up to 10 days. Serve with roast chicken, grilled lamb, or alongside cheese, or use to top a burger or roast beef sandwich. You can even use these onions as the base for a stew (add browned pieces of beef or lamb, a few diced root vegetables, and a bit of water or stock and simmer until the meat is incredibly tender).

Champagne + Honey Poached Pears: Peel and core pears that aren't too ripe (otherwise they won't hold their shape) and poach in Champagne that you've brought to a simmer and sweetened gently with honey. Cook just until tender and then remove the pears from the poaching liquid. Reduce the liquid over high heat to a syrup and drizzle on the pears. Serve as is or with unsweetened whipped cream, plain yogurt, sour cream, or vanilla ice cream. Also very good with pound cake or other plain cake.

Red Wine–Poached Eggs: Poach eggs in red wine instead of water for added color and flavor. If you'd like a more complex dish, start by crisping some diced bacon in a large pot and remove with a slotted spoon. Add tons of sliced mushrooms to the bacon fat and soften them over the heat. Add red wine to cover and simmer until slightly concentrated and then poach eggs in the mixture. Serve with the mushrooms on garlic-rubbed toast or soft polenta.

Seven Things to Do with Cooked Rice

Biryani-Style Fried Rice: For four servings, in a large nonstick skillet over medium-high heat, melt 3 Tbsp ghee or unsalted butter. Add a finely diced yellow onion, about 1 Tbsp peeled and minced or grated fresh ginger, and 3 minced garlic cloves. Cook, stirring, until the vegetables are softened, about 10 minutes. Add 1 Tbsp ground turmeric and ½ tsp each salt, ground cinnamon, and ground cardamom. Stir the spices into the aromatics and cook just until they're fragrant, about 30 seconds. Add 3 to 4 cups [480 to 640 g] cooked rice (any kind) and cook, stirring, until the rice is warmed through, 1 to 2 minutes. Season to taste with salt. Add a large handful of toasted sliced almonds and golden raisins (or chopped dried apricots). Transfer to a serving platter or bowl and top with a handful of roughly chopped fresh cilantro. Serve warm, preferably with plain yogurt and a bowl of Cilantro + Coconut Chutney (page 19) for spooning on top.

Paella-Style Fried Rice: For four servings, in a large nonstick skillet over medium-high heat, warm 2 Tbsp olive oil. Add a finely diced yellow onion, 4 minced garlic cloves, and a small handful of thinly sliced cured chorizo (if you are a vegetarian, skip the chorizo and add a heaping tsp of pimentón [smoked Spanish paprika]). Cook, stirring, until the onion has softened and the chorizo is crisp, about 10 minutes. Meanwhile, put a large pinch of saffron threads into a small bowl with 3 Tbsp boiling water and let steep. Add ½ lb [230] shrimp, peeled and deveined, to the skillet, sprinkle generously with salt, and cook, flipping the shrimp once, until browned on both sides, about 1½ minutes per side. Add 3 to 4 cups [480 to 640 g] cooked rice (any kind) and a handful of frozen peas to the skillet. Cook, stirring, until the rice is warmed through and the peas are tender, 1 to 2 minutes. Drizzle the saffron mixture on top and stir well to combine. Season the rice to taste with salt. Transfer to a serving platter or bowl and serve immediately.

Lox + Eggs Fried Rice: For four servings, in a large nonstick skillet over medium-high heat, warm 2 Tbsp olive oil. Add 2 small diced yellow onions and cook, stirring now and then, until the onions are softened, about 10 minutes. Add ¼ lb [115 g] roughly chopped lox and 3 to 4 cups [480 to 640 g] cooked rice (any kind) and cook, stirring, until the rice is warmed through, 1 to 2 minutes. Add 3 lightly beaten eggs and cook, stirring constantly, until the eggs are just set. Season to taste with pepper and salt (you might not need any salt, depending on the saltiness of the lox). Transfer to a serving platter or bowl and top with a handful of thinly sliced scallions. Serve immediately.

Avocado Hand Rolls: For each hand roll, cut a standard sheet of toasted nori seaweed in half lengthwise. Lay it, shiny-side down and with a short side facing you, on your work surface. Place about 2 heaping Tbsp room-temperature cooked rice (any kind) on the bottom third of the nori and then top with a few slices of ripe avocado, a pinch of toasted sesame seeds, and some matchsticks of cucumber and/or carrot. Roll on a slight diagonal to form a cone. Repeat the process to make as many hand rolls as you like. Serve with a mixture of equal parts mayonnaise, red chile paste, soy sauce, and water for dipping.

Simplest Bibimbap: For four servings, warm 2 Tbsp olive oil in a medium non-stick skillet over medium heat. Add 3 to 4 cups [480 to 640 g] cooked rice (any kind) and sprinkle with a large pinch of salt. Cook, stirring now and then, until the rice is heated through. Divide the rice among four shallow bowls and top each serving with a small handful each chopped cabbage kimchi, thinly sliced cucumbers, and cooked greens (like spinach or kale, which can be just steamed or wilted with ginger and garlic). Fry 4 eggs in the now-empty pan and top each serving with one. Serve immediately.

Vietnamese Comfort Soup: For four servings, put 8 cups [2 L] chicken stock into a large pot along with 2 heaping Tbsp peeled and minced or grated fresh ginger, 4 crushed garlic cloves, a star anise pod, 2 whole dried cloves, one 2-in [5-cm] cinnamon stick, and a small square of dried kombu seaweed. Simmer for 30 minutes and then strain the stock (discard the solids) and return it to the pot along with 3 Tbsp fish sauce and 1 tsp sugar. Season to taste with salt and pepper. Add 1½ cups [240 g] cooked rice (any kind) and simmer until the rice is hot. Serve topped with roughly chopped fresh cilantro and thinly sliced jalapeño chile.

Brown Sugar Rice Pudding: For six generous servings, in a medium saucepan, combine 2 cups [320 g] cooked rice (any kind), 2 cups [480 ml] whole milk, and a large pinch of salt and cook over medium heat, stirring now and then, until quite creamy, about 15 minutes. Add ½ cup [120 ml] more whole milk, ½ cup [100 g] packed dark brown sugar, and 1 lightly beaten egg and stir vigorously to incorporate everything. Turn off the heat and add 1 tsp vanilla extract and 1 Tbsp unsalted butter and stir again quite vigorously. Serve warm, or cover with plastic wrap (press it directly on the surface to prevent a skin from forming) and let cool to room temperature, then refrigerate until ice-cold and serve cold. You can add raisins or other chopped dried fruit if you like (if you do, add along with the second addition of milk).

Seven Things to Do with Typical Takeout Leftovers

Spicy Mu Shu Omelet: Leftover mu shu filling (vegetables, pork, chicken—whatever) is one of the best things that ever happened to an omelet. For a single serving, I like to start by sautéing a little minced or grated fresh ginger and garlic (about 1 tsp each) in a splash of neutral oil (like canola or vegetable) in a small nonstick skillet. Once they're fragrant, add a large handful of the filling and cook, stirring, until warm and crisp in spots, about 2 minutes. Hit the mixture with a bit of minced fresh red chile (or a spoonful of red chile paste) and then transfer it to a small bowl. Beat together 2 eggs and pour them into the pan. Cook, stirring, until the bottom is just set, about 1½ minutes. Put the warm filling mixture on top and cover the skillet until the eggs are just cooked through, about 30 seconds. Slide half of the omelet onto a plate and fold over the other half to form a semicircle. Serve immediately. A thinly sliced scallion is a nice thing to sprinkle on top.

Warm Edamame Succotash: Shell leftover edamame. For every handful of the soybeans, cut the kernels off of an ear of corn and cut a handful of cherry tomatoes in half. Melt a small knob of butter in a skillet over medium-high heat. Add the corn and cook, stirring now and then, until bright yellow and tender, about

2 minutes, depending on how fresh your corn is. Add the edamame and cherry tomatoes and season with salt and pepper. Cook, stirring, until just warm. If you like, add a splash of soy sauce. Serve warm. Excellent with a fried or poached egg on top for breakfast or alongside grilled fish or chicken for lunch or dinner.

Cheesy Spaghetti Pie: Generously butter a large round cake pan. Put about 1 lb [455 g] spaghetti that you've cooked and sauced (with anything!) into a large bowl along with 3 lightly beaten eggs and a large handful each coarsely grated mozzarella and finely grated Parmesan cheese. Mix well to combine. Transfer the mixture to the prepared cake pan and bake in a 425°F [220°C] oven until the mixture is set, no raw egg clings to a paring knife inserted in the center, and the cheese is bubbling, about 40 minutes. For a crisp top, run the spaghetti pie under the broiler for a minute or two. Cut into wedges and serve.

Soy Sauce Almonds: Do you have a bunch of soy sauce packets in a kitchen drawer somewhere? Drizzle the soy sauce over raw almonds (for every handful of almonds, use about 2 tsp soy sauce) and mix well to combine. Spread the almonds on a sheet pan and roast in a 200°F [95°C] oven, stirring now and then, until dry and crisp, about 2 hours. Let the nuts cool at room temperature (they will continue to crisp as they cool) and then enjoy as a snack. These are especially good with cocktails or cold beer.

Spicy Pizza "Croutons": Cut leftover pizza into bite-size pieces, sprinkle with red pepper flakes, and broil until hot and bubbling. Use to top any hefty salad (Caesar salad is particularly good). The combination of cold, crunchy salad and hot (temperature and spice!) bites of pizza is sublime.

Waffled Fries (Not Waffle Fries): Put leftover French fries into your waffle maker not only to warm them up but also to crisp them. They're like the best hash browns you've ever had but without all of the work. This is best done with a waffle maker that has plates you can remove and put into the dishwasher (trust me on this). Serve with whatever you would normally dip fries in (ketchup, mayonnaise, barbecue sauce, or may I highly recommend the Buttermilk Ranch Dressing on page 96).

Chicken Tikka Tacos: Use leftover chicken tikka masala as the jumping-off point for tacos. Serve on warm corn tortillas (see page 230 for directions on how to warm) and top with thinly sliced red cabbage that you've scrunched with fresh lime juice and salt and then with plenty of fresh cilantro and/or with Cilantro + Coconut Chutney (page 19). Delicious.

Seven Things to Do with Leftover Snacks

Pretzel Chicken with Mustard Sauce:
Pulse leftover pretzels in a food processor until they're coarsely ground (or put them into a plastic bag and smash them with a mallet or a heavy pan). Dredge chicken tenders in flour that you've seasoned with salt and pepper, dip them in egg wash (1 or 2 eggs whisked with a spoonful of mustard and a splash of water), and then coat them with the pretzel crumbs. Place them on an oiled sheet pan and roast in a 425°F [220°C] oven, turning once, until browned and crisp and cooked through, 8 to 10 minutes per side. Mix equal parts mayonnaise or sour cream, Dijon mustard, and whole-grain mustard and season to taste with salt and pepper. Serve the chicken with the sauce.

Green Papaya Salad with Beef Jerky: Peel and shred a large green papaya (or substitute a green mango or even a couple of green apples). Dress with equal parts rice vinegar, fish sauce, and fresh lime juice and season to taste with salt and sugar. Add a handful each roughly chopped beef jerky, fresh cilantro, and fresh Thai basil. The beef jerky adds that special something!

Potato Chip Tortilla Española: I think it's probably pretty clear that I'm not really a molecular gastronomy type of gal, but I actually first read about this in a Ferran Adrià (of elBulli fame) cookbook. He suggested using potato chips in a *tortilla española* (which is essentially a potato frittata) instead of peeling and frying potatoes. I am all for a shortcut, especially one that involves a bag of potato chips. To make the tortilla, preheat your broiler. In a large bowl, whisk together 8 eggs, season with plenty of salt and pepper, and then stir in 3 cups [140 g] lightly crushed potato chips (the thicker the better). Let the chips sit in the egg for about 5 minutes to soften. In a large broiler-safe nonstick skillet over medium-high heat, warm 2 Tbsp olive oil. Add the egg mixture and cook just until the underside begins to set, about 3 minutes. Transfer the skillet to the hot broiler and cook just until the eggs are set throughout (test by shaking the pan) and the top is golden brown, about 5 minutes. Let the tortilla cool down for at least 10 minutes before cutting into wedges and serving. It's equally great at room temperature.

Macaroni + Cheese with Cheese Cracker Topping: Top macaroni and cheese with crushed cheese crackers before baking in a 350°F [180°C] oven for about 15 minutes to warm up the pasta and crisp the crackers. They make for an irresistibly cheesy, crunchy topping. My go-to macaroni and cheese is Preeti Mistry's Tikka Masala Macaroni and Cheese in *Feed the Resistance*. I can't recommend it highly enough.

Baked Eggs with Salsa: Place a thin layer of leftover salsa in the bottom of a baking dish (a pie plate or pan works well). Use a spoon to make as many indentations in the salsa as you have eggs to cook. Crack an egg into each indentation (the eggs can touch one another, but you want them in a single layer, so no overlapping). Season the eggs with salt and pepper. Bake in a 400°F [200°C] oven until the salsa is bubbling and the eggs are cooked through, about 10 minutes. Sprinkle with thinly sliced scallions and roughly chopped fresh cilantro and serve immediately. A drizzle of Lime + Hot Sauce Crema (page 232) is also really nice.

Crispy Popcorn Treats: Think of extra popcorn like it's Rice Krispies and substitute it for the cereal in the classic treats. To make them, put 4 Tbsp [55 g] unsalted butter (or coconut oil) into a large pot with one 10-oz [280-g] bag marshmallows and set over medium-low heat. Stir until the butter and marshmallows melt together in an incredibly messy mixture. Add 6 large handfuls of popped popcorn and a generous sprinkle of flaky salt (it makes a big difference!) and stir well to combine. Once the mixture is cool enough to handle, coat your hands with a little bit of butter or oil (this will keep the popcorn from sticking too much) and shape handfuls into round balls roughly the size of baseballs. Let the popcorn balls cool to room temperature before serving.

Spicy Peanuts with Garlic, Chile + Lime: In a medium nonstick skillet over medium heat, warm 1 Tbsp canola or other neutral oil. Add a minced garlic clove, 1 cup [140 g] roasted peanuts, a heaping Tbsp of red chile paste (preferably sambal oelek), and a large pinch of salt. Cook, stirring, until very fragrant and sizzling, about 1 minute. Turn off the heat and squeeze over the juice of ½ lime (use the other half for some cold beers, which go so well with these peanuts). Transfer to a serving dish and serve warm.

Seven Things to Do with Not-So-New Produce

Herb Stem Salsa Verde: When you've used up the leaves from tender herbs like parsley and cilantro, don't just toss the stems. They have tons of flavor! Use them in stock or turn them into something tasty like this salsa. To make it, very thinly mince the stems. For every handful, add a minced garlic clove, a small handful of drained brined capers that you've run your knife through, and a spoonful of Dijon mustard. If you love anchovies like I do, add a couple of minced olive oil–packed fillets. Add a splash of red or white wine vinegar and enough olive oil to turn the mixture into a sauce (about ¼ cup/60 ml should be about right). Season to taste with salt and pepper. Serve on boiled eggs, roasted potatoes, grilled chicken or fish, seared scallops, or broiled lamb—basically, anything.

Dried Rosemary Salt: When you have a bit too much rosemary, dry it at room temperature or in a 200°F [95°C] oven until dry and crisp and then strip the leaves from the stems. For every small handful of leaves, use 2 large handfuls of kosher salt, put both into a food processor, and pulse until the rosemary is finely chopped and mixed evenly with the salt. Store in a tightly capped jar in a dark spot at room temperature. Use whenever salt and rosemary would also be welcome (so on root vegetables or chicken before roasting, pork tenderloin or steak before grilling, or mushrooms as they're sautéing). It makes a lovely gift, too.

Shaved Celery + Parmesan Salad: When you have too much celery, or celery that is just beginning to lose its crispness, thinly slice it on the diagonal with either a very sharp knife or carefully on a mandoline. Dress the celery with equal parts lemon juice and extra-virgin olive oil and season to taste with salt and pepper. Serve topped with shaved Parmesan cheese and an extra drizzle of olive oil. Toasted and chopped hazelnuts are also very nice on this.

Whole Wheat Blackberry Pancakes: When blackberries (or any berries) aren't looking too perky, just add them to these easy pancakes. For two generous servings, beat 2 eggs with 1 cup [240 ml] buttermilk, 1 Tbsp maple syrup, 1 tsp vanilla extract, and ½ tsp each salt, baking soda, ground cinnamon, and ground ginger. Stir in ½ cup [70 g] whole wheat flour. Spoon the batter into a hot buttered skillet (or try coconut oil or ghee) to form pancakes and top with blackberries. Flip when the undersides are browned and then cook until the second sides are browned and the blackberries are lightly caramelized. Serve with whipped cream and crushed blackberries or blackberry jam.

Onion + Garlic Broth: Onions and garlic that are past their prime (or that you have in excess) can be roughly chopped, skins and all, and put into a large pot with water to cover. Season generously with salt and simmer until the onions and garlic have lost all of their structural integrity and the broth is very aromatic, at least 1 hour but preferably 2 hours. Strain and use immediately, or let cool to room temperature and store in airtight containers in the refrigerator for up to 1 week or freeze for up to 6 months. Serve as is with tiny pasta and grated cheese for a simple but satisfying soup, or use in any dish that calls for chicken or vegetable stock (so soups, risottos, braises, and the like). You can also add caramelized onions and garlic to the broth and serve as a simple onion soup.

Homemade Hot Sauce: When you have grown or purchased too many hot chiles, discard the stems, roughly chop the chiles, and put them into a small saucepan. Cover with equal parts water and distilled white vinegar. For every 1 cup [240 ml] liquid, add 1 tsp each salt and sugar. Simmer until the chiles are softened, about 15 minutes. Use an immersion blender to purée the mixture (or transfer to a countertop blender or food processor). Season to taste with more salt if needed. If you prefer a really smooth sauce, strain through a fine-mesh sieve. Serve at room temperature. Leftovers can be stored in a tightly capped jar in the refrigerator for up to 2 weeks. When handling hot chiles, be careful to avoid touching your eyes or other sensitive areas.

Banana Bread Milkshake: When you have overripe bananas and don't feel like baking, peel them and then freeze them. For each serving, put a frozen banana into the blender with ½ cup [120 ml] milk (any kind), ½ tsp each ground cinnamon and vanilla extract, and a small handful of walnuts. Purée until smooth and enjoy immediately for all of the flavors of banana bread without any of the baking.

Seven Things to Bring
When You're Invited to Dinner

A Bottle of Really Good Olive Oil:
Although wine is usually the go-to bottle
to carry to someone's house, I highly
recommend swapping it out for olive oil.
It's a little unexpected but so highly useful
for any person who loves to cook. Plus
the price range and variety of options are
pretty much the same as wine.

Bread + Salt: It's been a longstanding
tradition in my family (and many others
with Eastern European roots) to bring
bread and salt as gifts when visiting
friends or family in their new home. The
combination has symbolized hospitality
for a long time. I like picking up a great
loaf from a bakery and tying a ribbon
around high-quality salt, like a box of
Maldon or a jar of Jacobsen.

Granola + Freshly Squeezed Orange Juice:
When invited for dinner, instead of adding
to an already planned meal, I love bringing
stuff for a great breakfast. You can make
your own granola (I highly recommend the
Coconut + Almond Granola in *Feed the
Resistance*) or buy a bag of something great
like Early Bird Granola (made in Brooklyn
by a woman-owned business).

Challah, a Dozen Eggs + Maple Syrup:
Along the same lines as the granola and
orange juice suggestion, bring over a loaf
of challah, a dozen farm-fresh eggs, and
a bottle of good maple syrup. You will
be setting up your hosts for French toast
success.

**A Bag of Really Good Coffee Beans +
a Couple of Beautiful Mugs:** Can't go
wrong with this combination. For coffee,
get whatever you swear by, and for mugs, I
highly suggest Nicholas Newcomb's Hudson Valley Camp Mugs (www.nicholasnewcomb.com).

**Fox's U-Bet Syrup, Milk in a Glass
Bottle, Bubbly Seltzer:** Bring stuff for
egg creams to have that evening or for
your hosts to enjoy another time. It's fun
and totally unexpected but also sort of
familiar, just like everything I adore in the
kitchen (and in life in general).

Donation to a Local Food Pantry:
For every meal you share with friends,
wouldn't it be great to provide a meal
(or a few) for someone without the same
access? Food pantries are located in just
about every neighborhood. Look up the
one closest to the home you'll be visiting
and donate in your host's name. Honestly,
one of the best gifts Grace and I ever
received was from our friends Lacey and
Michelle after they spent a weekend at our
house. They wrote a check to Angel Food
East, an organization for which Grace
and I volunteer every week, cooking with
a group that provides meals for folks in
our community who are homebound with
chronic illnesses. That gift was better than
any scented candle or bottle of wine.

Seven Great Things to Delegate

Ice: You can never have too much when you're having a group over, and unless you have a very large freezer, it's a hard item to get ahead of time. Ask someone to pick up a bag or two on his or her way over and cross it off your list.

Dinner the Night Before a Holiday and/or Breakfast the Day of the Holiday: When you are having a crowd for a holiday or any large gathering, it can be difficult to muster enough bandwidth to plan for the meals around *the meal*. Assign these to your family and friends. It could be as simple as having someone else order pizza the night before or take care of coffee, toast, and eggs in the morning.

Flowers: Have someone else bring them and arrange them. Done and done.

Setting the Table: In my house, my passion is all about what's on the plate and in the bowls. As for which plates and which bowls, I'm more indecisive. Luckily I grew up with a father who is passionate about table settings and married a woman who is, too. Delegating the table to one of them always means I get to do what I love and vice versa.

Music: One of the best things a friend can bring over is an excellent playlist. Explain the mood you want to set for the evening and let her or him run with it.

Alcohol: For friends and family who don't love to cook (or if you do indeed want to cook everything), assign the booze and be specific about what you want (for example, *cold* beer or a particular type of tequila for margaritas). A bonus of this suggestion is that alcohol is normally the most expensive part of any meal and delegating it means you can offset the cost of having people over, which will hopefully encourage you to have people over more often.

Trash: When I lived for so many years in New York City, I always offered to take the trash downstairs when I was leaving a friend's apartment after dinner. If you live in a big city, especially one with a lot of walk-up apartments, you know eliminating the need to make that trip down and back up the stairs is a small victory for your host.

Recipes by Type

Spicy Pozole 188

Creamy Cauliflower + Lettuce Soup 199

Chilled Cucumber + Yogurt Soup 249

Vietnamese Comfort Soup 269

Onion + Garlic Broth 275

COOKED VEGETABLES

Stuffed Peppers 61

String Beans with Toasted Almonds + Lemon 74

Spicy Stir-Fried Lettuce + Celery with Garlic 99

Charred Broccoli with Capers + Lemon 106

Double-Baked Potatoes with Horseradish + Cheddar 107

Crispy, Cheesy Potato Cakes 113

Roasted Fennel + Endive 123

Roasted Red Cabbage with Anchovy + Pinenuts 123

Stir-Fried Roasted Eggplant with Pork 133

Baby Bok Choy with Sesame Sauce 134

Crushed Potatoes + Peas 144

Sautéed Zucchini with Green Goddess Dressing 145

Sweet Potato Oven Fries with Comeback Sauce 156

Crispy Tofu + Asparagus Stir-Fry 177

Creamy Garlic Mashed Cauliflower 195

Kale + Mushroom Taco Filling 228

Chorizo + Potato Taco Filling 229

Grilled Okra + Corn with Lemon + Red Chile 244

Warm Edamame Succotash 270

Waffled Fries (Not Waffle Fries) 271

SAUCES + DIPS

Mango Chutney 24

Arugula + Lemon Pesto 39

Beet Dip 61

Apple Cider Gravy 70

Roasted Applesauce 77

Bagna Cauda with Endive + Fennel 118

Bagna Cauda Caesar Dressing 123

Zucchini Hummus 149

Golden Beet + Horseradish Relish 171

Pineapple Salsa 188

Eggplant Dip 213

Broccoli Rabe Pesto 221

Lime + Hot Sauce Crema 232

Charred Tomatillo + Scallion Salsa 233

Greek Yogurt with Fried Pistachios + Lemon 255

Red Wine Onions 265

Herb Stem Salsa Verde 274

Dried Rosemary Salt 274

Homemade Hot Sauce 275

POULTRY + MEAT

Garlic Toast Meatballs 39

Chicken + Roasted Tomato Enchiladas 44

Celebration Chicken with Sweet Potatoes + Dates 54

Coronation Chicken Salad 61

Roast Turkey Breast + Onions with Mustard + Sage 68

Shredded Turkey, String Beans + Cucumbers with Soy + Ginger 77

Chicken + Black-Eyed Pea Chili 92

Simplest Pulled Pork with Vinegar Slaw 153

Cuban Sandwiches 161

Aunt Sharon's Brisket with Carrots 168

Confetti Meatloaf 194

Open-Faced Meatloaf Melts 199

Grilled Vietnamese Flank Steak 204

Steak + Kimchi Quesadillas 213

Lamb Burgers with Grilled Red Onions 242

Grilled Beef + Zucchini Meatballs with Tahini Dressing 257

Meatball Pita Sandwiches 261

Braised Pork with Red Wine + Cherries 264

Coq au Vin Blanc 264

Chicken Tikka Tacos 271

Pretzel Chicken with Mustard Sauce 272

FISH + SHELLFISH

Garlicky Shrimp with Tequila + Lime 42

Crab Toasts with Lemon + Red Chile 117

Spaghetti with Scallops, Squid + Shrimp 119

Crab Cakes 123

Korean-Style Cold Seafood Salad 123

Oven-Steamed Fish with Crispy Garlic + Red Chile Oil 130

Striped Bass with Butter Verde 142

Doug's Fish Salad 149

RICE + GRAINS + PASTA + BREADS

Whole Wheat + Cumin Flatbreads 21

Flatbread Pizza 24

Italian Flag Baked Pasta 33

Baked Saffron Rice 55

Sheet Pan Bread Stuffing with Sausage + Spinach 71

Squash Grilled Cheese 77

Little Cabbage Hand Pies 89

Skillet Cornbread with Cheddar + Scallions 93

Cornbread Stuffing 99

Penne ai Fungi 113

Fish + Crispy Garlic Fried Rice 135

Cold Rice Noodle + Bok Choy Salad 135

Charoset Quinoa 174

Arroz con Pollo 188

Lettuce + Spring Pea Risotto 199

Pressed Broccoli Rabe + Mozzarella Sandwiches 217

Broccoli Rabe + Farro Salad 221

Drunken Spaghetti 264

Biryani-Style Fried Rice 268

Paella-Style Fried Rice 268

Lox + Eggs Fried Rice 268

Simplest Bibimbap 269

Cheesy Spaghetti Pie 270

Spicy Pizza "Croutons" 271

Macaroni and Cheese with Cheese Cracker Topping 272

DESSERTS + BAKED GOODS

Mango with Cardamom Syrup + Pistachios 23

Polenta + Nutella Sandwich Cookies 38

Toasted Coconut Cake 47

Applesauce Cake with Cream Cheese + Honey Frosting 58

Maple Roasted Apples with Vanilla Ice Cream + Roasted Pecans 75

Easy Pumpkin + Olive Oil Cake 76

Spiced Banana Brown Bread 85

Easiest Cantaloupe Sorbet 89

Caramelized Bananas with Sour Cream + Brown Sugar 98

Black Forest Cake 108

Boozy Lemon Pound Cake 123

Pistachio Mandelbrot Cookies 148

Healthy, Happy Wife Cake 158

Lazy Vanilla Semifreddo with Honeyed Strawberries 176

Pineapple with Homemade Tajín 187

Raspberries with Cocoa Whipped Cream 197

Vietnamese Iced Coffee Granita 213

Hikers' Cookies 220

Easy Nectarine Crumble 221

Whole Wheat Berry Shortcakes 246

Burger Bun Summer Pudding 249

Yogurt Cake with Fig Preserves 259

Champagne + Honey Poached Pears 265

Brown Sugar Rice Pudding 269

Crispy Popcorn Treats 273

DRINKS

Jody's Plum Bibonade 36

Maple Syrup Old-Fashioneds 102

Boozy Lemon Slushies 122

Easiest Almond Horchata 181

Vietnamese Iced Coffee 211

Pineapple Margaritas 234

Frozen Watermelon Aguas Frescas 238

Sangria Ice Cubes 264

Banana Bread Milkshake 275

Even More Menu Suggestions

BREAKFASTS

1. Whole Wheat Blackberry Pancakes (page 274) / *fresh orange juice*

2. Taco Filling Hash (page 235) / *poached eggs / hot coffee*

3. Spicy Mu Shu Omelet (page 270) / Vietnamese Iced Coffee (page 211)

4. Baked Eggs with Salsa (page 273) / *warm corn tortillas / watermelon*

5. Banana Bread French Toast (page 89) / *hot chocolate*

LUNCHES

1. Meatball Pita Sandwiches (page 261) / *sliced cucumbers with dill and vinegar*

2. Creamy Cauliflower + Lettuce Soup (page 199) / *grilled cheese sandwiches*

3. Iceberg Wedge Salad with Pickled Shallots (page 105) / *grilled chicken*

4. Cuban Sandwiches (page 161) / *cold beer*

5. Grilled Vietnamese Flank Steak (page 204) / *cold rice noodles / sliced cucumbers*

COCKTAILS + NOSHES

1. Maple Syrup Old-Fashioneds (page 102) / Bagna Cauda with Endive + Fennel (page 118)

2. Boozy Lemon Slushies (page 122) / bites of Potato Chip Tortilla Española (page 272)

3. Jody's Plum Bibonade (page 36) / Eggplant Dip (page 213) / *toasted pita*

4. Pineapple Margaritas (page 234) / Steak + Kimchi Quesadillas (page 213)

5. *Sangria* with Sangria Ice Cubes (page 264) / Simplest + Best Nachos (page 180)

DINNERS

1. Crab Toasts with Lemon + Red Chile (page 117) / *spaghetti* with Broccoli Rabe Pesto (page 221)

2. Celebration Chicken with Sweet Potatoes + Dates (page 54) / *arugula dressed with lemon juice and olive oil*

3. Braised Pork with Red Wine + Cherries (page 264) / Crushed Potatoes + Peas (page 144)

4. Shredded Cabbage Salad with Feta + Herbs (page 87) / *grilled shrimp*

5. Confetti Meatloaf (page 194) / String Beans with Toasted Almonds + Lemon (page 74)

A Few Notes on Tools + Ingredients

I don't have much to tell you about what tools and ingredients you need in your kitchen that you can't find in most cookbooks (including *Small Victories*) and on that fun thing called the Internet. My advice is *less is more* and a few good-quality things, whether equipment or groceries, are better than an abundance of just okay things.

When it comes to **TOOLS**, here are a few things I find indispensible beyond the usual chef's knife, large cutting board, and pots and pans.

SPIDER: This is somewhat like a wide sieve with a long handle. It is ideal for frying (like the tortillas for the Tortilla Soup with The Works on page 184), and it's great for pulling vegetables or pasta out of boiling

water. I also use mine as a sort of mini colander when I rinse off berries because it's right in the utensil crock on my counter, and I often can't be bothered to open a drawer or cabinet if I don't need to.

MICROPLANE GRATER: Nothing is better for grating citrus zest than a fine-rasp Microplane grater. I also use mine for finely grating fresh ginger rather than mincing it, as the grater works through all of the fibers so easily and leaves you with puréed ginger. It also makes quick work of garlic cloves and hard cheeses.

SHEET PANS: I would be lost without a stack of heavy-duty, affordable stainless-steel sheet pans. Sure they're great for roasting *anything*, but they're also great for carrying a bunch of things to the table or for taking with you to the grill to use as a landing pad for whatever you're cooking. I bought a stack of them about a decade ago at a restaurant supply store for very little money, use them every single day, and they're still going strong. Whenever I say "sheet pan" in this book (or anywhere, for that matter), I am referring to the shallow-rimmed pans labeled "half sheet pans" at restaurant supply stores (they're half the size of whole sheet pans, which are industrial size). They are confusingly described at stores and online as either 12 by 17 in [30.5 by 43 cm] or 13 by 18 in [33 by 46 cm]. The first measurement refers to the dimensions of the interior surface space of the sheet pan and the second is from the outside edge to the outside edge.

LARGE, STURDY SPATULA FOR GRILLING: Speaking of the grill, I can't say enough good things about a sturdy metal spatula for grilling. First, there's something about assertively sliding one underneath whatever you're cooking that feels satisfyingly defiant. Second, it guarantees you don't leave the crust of whatever you're grilling—burgers, planks of eggplant, chicken breasts—on the grate, unlike when you try to pry it off with tongs. Don't get me wrong, I rely on TONGS like an extra set of hands. Have both on you and you'll be golden.

DISHES: Grace and I have lots of old family dishes and are always buying fun ceramics. We'd much rather have something unfortunately break while we're using it than let it collect dust in a cabinet because we're afraid of using it. Life is short: eat on real plates that mean something to you!

When it comes to INGREDIENTS, if I cannot find something within a half hour of my house (I live in a small, rural town), it will either not appear in my recipes or I will give you an explanation for why I think it's worth seeking out, plus some ideas for easy-to-find substitutions. I cook every single day, and I prefer to spend that time in the kitchen rather than crisscrossing town(s) to shop at multiple stores. I strongly believe that simple, readily available ingredients are all you need to make great food. Here are some notes and thoughts on a few ingredients that appear in the book that might not already be in your kitchen.

EGGS, YOGURT, BUTTER, ONIONS: First, just a note on these staples. I tested the recipes in this book with large eggs, full-fat yogurt, unsalted butter, and medium onions. Unless otherwise noted, these sizes and descriptions should be assumed throughout.

ANCHOVIES: I use olive oil–packed anchovy fillets from Ortiz. They're a little expensive compared with some other brands, but a few anchovies go a long way, and when it comes to something this strong in flavor, it's good to choose high quality.

CHILE PASTES: I can't always find fresh red chiles, so I use a lot of chile paste in my cooking. It provides not only the same heat as fresh chiles but also means you don't have to chop anything. Plus, it usually contains some other assertive ingredients, like garlic and vinegar, which add even more flavor. My preferred chile pastes are the Cherry Pepper Spread from Gordy's Pickle Jar and any brand of sambal oelek (most of them come with a green top).

FISH SAUCE: Funky (in a good way) and salty, fish sauce is indispensible as far as I am concerned! I use it anytime I make Vietnamese food (such as the Grilled Vietnamese Flank Steak on page 204 or the Warm Grilled Eggplant + Tomato Salad with Herbs on page 208). Red Boat is the brand I trust and like the best.

FRUIT PRESERVES: I always reach for Bonne Maman fruit preserves (including fig for the Yogurt Cake with Fig Preserves on page 259 and cherry for the Black Forest Cake on page 109), plus the jars are the best for reusing once the preserves are gone. I clean them and use them for making salad dressing or for storing things like random handfuls of leftover nuts.

KOSHER SALT: I use Diamond Crystal kosher salt in my kitchen, and it's what I used to test all of the recipes in this book. Morton's kosher salt is twice as salty, so if that's what you have on the shelf, add only half the amount called for in the recipes. Either way, season to taste as you go, as what tastes perfectly seasoned to me might not be the same for you, and that's okay!

OLIVE OIL: For daily cooking and for salad dressings and whatnot, my go-to olive oil brand is California Olive Ranch. It's delicious, not too expensive, and it's a brand you can trust (for a variety of reasons, including its sound environmental practices). Those are all surprisingly difficult qualities to find in olive oil land, especially in one company.

PEELED GARLIC: I use peeled garlic all of the time. Yes, it's not as fresh and flavorful as garlic you peel yourself, but if it means getting a meal on the table is more approachable, I say go for it. I find that folks always seem surprised when I tell them I use peeled garlic. But I do so unabashedly, and I figure it is worth sharing here. Always look for containers with whole cloves that aren't too bruised or "sweaty." Peeled garlic will keep pretty well for a while, as long as it's not wet. But once it's damp, it gets super stinky and strong in a not-wonderful way. One grocery store in my area (shout-out to Adams!) always has the best peeled garlic, and I go out of my way to buy it there. Find your garlic and get it. It'll put you one step closer to cooking.

PICKLED JALAPEÑO CHILES: One of my favorite ingredients in the world, pickled jalapeños add snap and pop to just about everything they touch. My preferred brand is Thai Basil Jalapeños from Gordy's Pickle Jar (I know I'm starting to sound like a broken record and, no, Gordy's doesn't pay me; I just love the company's products and Sarah and Sheila who make them!).

TAHINI: I love tahini (sesame seed paste) because it's loaded with flavor and makes everything it comes in contact with taste so rich. Soom is my preferred brand, hands down. It is consistently creamy and has unbelievably toasty flavor. Beyond that, it's run by three sisters, which is quite sweet, and they take great care in how they source and process the sesame seeds.

TOASTED SESAME OIL: Full of strong flavor, I use toasted sesame oil like a condiment rather than a cooking oil. My preferred brands are Kadoya (a funky glass bottle) and La Tourangelle (a cylindrical tin). Try to buy small bottles or tins, as the oil can go bad relatively quickly (store it in the refrigerator to prolong its freshness).

WHOLE WHEAT FLOUR: I love baking with whole wheat flour because it's more nutritious than white flour and it has a lot more flavor and dimension. My go-to brand is King Arthur.

Give Back + Do Good

As I wrote in *Small Victories*, this cookbook, like nearly every single cookbook out there, arrives in your hands with the assumption that you not only have leisurely time to read it but also the means to buy the ingredients if you feel like making a recipe and a safe place to cook and eat. Wouldn't it be wonderful if this were the case for everyone? Until it is, there's a lot we can all do (big things, small things, and everything in between) to help ensure there's a lot more equity at the table.

Food offers us many ways to give back and to do good. Here is a helpful list of ten ways to do a bit of both. I hope something on it grabs you and you give it a go, or maybe this list will inspire even more ideas. Food is about people and people are community. We're all in this life and this world together, and food is a tangible, wonderful way to connect and share.

TEACH: Show someone who doesn't know how to cook how to scramble eggs, make chicken soup, and roast vegetables. You will be teaching that person how to fish instead of just giving him or her fish. Feel free to throw a fish dish into the lesson or to suit the list of recipes to whatever your novice cook likes; just keep it easy and approachable. You will be helping someone to feed him- or herself and hopefully one or two family members or friends forever. It could be anyone: a college student, your own child, or even a friend's child. This simple act makes an enormous, empowering difference and has a true butterfly effect.

SHOW UP: If someone in your community is grieving or going through a difficult time of any kind (recovering from an illness, for example), drop off a comforting, homemade meal that's easy to heat and eat and include instructions on how to heat it. This also goes for anyone in your community with a new child (whether it's a newborn, a foster child in need of a temporary home, or a newly adopted kid going through a huge transition). Here are a few ideas for good dishes to share: Vietnamese Comfort Soup (page 269), Chicken + Roasted Tomato Enchiladas (page 44), Chicken + Black-Eyed Pea Chili (page 92), and Italian Flag Baked Pasta (page 33).

EDUCATE: Spend some time helping your local food bank and/or your local food pantry distribute food. Take a moment to share a recipe with the person receiving the food. This could be a brief verbal description ("hey, if you mix this rice with some of those frozen peas and an egg, you'll have a quick and easy fried rice") or consider making little recipe cards for some of the most commonly distributed items. Pairing a bit of inspiration with the ingredients goes a long way. Check out www.facebook.com/rochesterfoodpantry for some fun and easy videos that Grace and I made for our local food pantry and feel free to use them for yours.

ORGANIZE: Organize a community potluck and ask everyone you invite to bring someone new. Connect people. Do this in your home or at a local community or recreation center.

BAKE + SHARE: Bake something simple (I'm talking about you Applesauce Cake with Cream Cheese + Honey Frosting on page 58, Easy Pumpkin + Olive Oil Cake on page 76, Spiced Banana Brown Bread on page 85, and Hikers' Cookies on page 220) and take it to your local firehouse, police station, public library, emergency room, and/or the teachers' room at your public school and thank whoever you're giving it to for their service.

BAKE + SELL: Have a bake sale and give all of the proceeds to an organization that helps support something you believe in. A few ideas include Planned Parenthood (www.plannedparenthood.org), the American Civil Liberties Union (www.aclu.org), and the Southern Poverty Law Center (www.splcenter.org).

SUPPORT: Support food businesses that have social impact woven into their missions. A few great examples include Hot Bread Kitchen in Manhattan (www.hotbreadkitchen.org), which employs and trains women facing economic insecurity; Ovenly bakery in Brooklyn (www.oven.ly), which partners with Getting Out Staying Out and the Ansob Center for Refugees to provide jobs for young men who have been in the criminal justice system and for refugees, respectively; and La Cocina in San Francisco (www.lacocinasf.org), which helps cultivate low-income food entrepreneurs, specifically women from communities of color and immigrant communities. And if you don't live in New York or San Francisco, worry not. You can order products—they make great gifts—from all of these folks on their websites.

BUY: Buy cookbooks written by and featuring writers of color. It's an easy and tangible way to support more inclusive storytelling, plus you'll discover many amazing recipes. Here are a few recommendations. If you don't have one of Dr. Jessica B. Harris's many books, check one out (it's hard to choose from her collection, but I would suggest starting with *The Welcome Table* and also her memoir, *My Soul Looks Back*). A couple more to consider for your shelf are *Grandbaby Cakes* by Jocelyn Delk Adams and *The Back in the Day Bakery Cookbook* by Cheryl and Griffith Day, two of the best baking books. Also, *The Up South Cookbook* by Nicole Taylor, *Cooking Solo* by Klancy Miller, *Senegal* by Pierre Thiam, *The Juhu Beach Club Cookbook* by Preeti Mistry, *The Jemima Code* by Toni Tipton-Martin, *Afro-Vegan* by Bryant Terry, *Salt, Fat, Acid, Heat* by Samin Nosrat, *Season* by Nik Sharma, and *The Saffron Tales* by Yasmin Khan.

VOTE: Make sure everyone who comes to your house to eat a meal is registered to vote. Help them register if they're not. Host a dinner party on an election day (whether it's national or local), invite your neighbors over, and make it an event. It helps to have something on the calendar as both a reminder and an incentive.

ASK: Whether you're cooking a meal at home or going out to a restaurant, choose a dish from a culture you don't know much about and read about it and ask questions. I have devoted my whole life to food, and I learn something new every single day, which is why I love what I do and never get bored. That we all have so much we can learn is a huge, beautiful gift.

Acknowledgments

An enormous **thank you** to:

The incredibly capable, supportive folks at Chronicle Books. Thanks especially to Sarah Billingsley, Vanessa Dina, Albee Dalbotten, Alexandra Brown, Marie Oishi, Tera Killip, Christine Carswell, and Tyrrell Mahoney. I love making books with you.

Kari Stuart for taking care of all of the things that stress me out so I can just do what I love. I know how rare it is to be able to say and do that. And to Cat Shook for keeping all of the pieces moving.

Marisa Dobson for coming on board and working so hard.

David Loftus, Tyna Hoang, and Caroline Lange for your talent, kindness, and support. Thank you from the bottom of my heart.

Rebecca Bartoshesky for making an exception to help me out!

Jen May for stepping in. Cheers to upstate!

Amelia Lang for showing up in such a kind way. And thanks for this photo right here! Thank you also to Fabio Chizzola and Laura Ferrara, and to Elise Kornack and Anna Hieronimus for bringing over the most beautiful berries.

My amazing "Kitchen Cabinet" for testing so many of these recipes while I was figuring them out and for your helpful, supportive, insightful feedback: Elaine Bonney, Grace Bonney, Cleo Brock-Abraham, Steph Dietz-Urena, Julie Gigax, Anne Heinrich, Amelia Lang, Natalie Marquis, Julie Kohn, Lizzy May Oates, Kate Rodenhouse, Lacey Soslow + Michelle Landry, Kari Stuart + Nic Newcomb, Kait Turshen, Natasha Warner, and Marsha Winters. And thanks to Nicole Taylor for her extremely valuable insight.

My neighbors for willingly accepting so many odd care packages as I worked my way through the recipes, especially the Kingston chapter of Citizen Action and Tanya Miszko Kefer (who also consistently provides the most positive space for turning work off).

Susan, my therapist, thank you. Mental health is wealth!

Mom and Dad for always being such helpful sounding boards. Dad (and Steve!), thank you so much for designing the proposal and helping me hit the ground running. Thank you also for letting me borrow so many of your dishes and linens—the ones that mean so much to me—and for showing up in all of the ways you do.

All of my family and to my friends who are also my family. Having you around the table is always the best part of any meal.

My darling Grace, I love you beyond the moon. And to Hope, Winky, and Turk. I am the luckiest girl in the world.

Index